Wounds That Heal

Wounds That Heal

*The Importance of Church Discipline within
Balthasar Hubmaier's Theology*

SIMON VICTOR GONCHARENKO

☙PICKWICK *Publications* · Eugene, Oregon

WOUNDS THAT HEAL
The Importance of Church Discipline within Balthasar Hubmaier's Theology

Copyright © 2012 Simon Victor Goncharenko. All rights reserved. Except for brief quotations in critical publications or reviews, no part of this book may be reproduced in any manner without prior written permission from the publisher. Write: Permissions, Wipf and Stock Publishers, 199 W. 8th Ave., Suite 3, Eugene, OR 97401.

Pickwick Publications
An Imprint of Wipf and Stock Publishers
199 W. 8th Ave., Suite 3
Eugene, OR 97401

www.wipfandstock.com

ISBN 13: 978-1-61097-604-6

Cataloging-in-Publication data:

Goncharenko, Simon Victor.

> Wounds that heal : the importance of church discipline within Balthasar Hubmaier's theology / Simon Victor Goncharenko.
>
> xiv + 150 p. ; 23 cm. Includes bibliographical references and index.
>
> ISBN 13: 978-1-61097-604-6
>
> 1. Hubmaier, Balthasar, d. 1528. 2. Church discipline. 3. Anabaptists—Doctrines—History—16th century—Sources. I. Title.

BX4946.H8 G76 2012

Manufactured in the U.S.A.

To my wife, Alice—my fellow heir of the grace of life (1 Pet 3:7), whose sacrifices, flexibility, and quiet devotion to our family and strength in the Lord cannot be expressed in words. Your lasting beauty of gentle and tranquil spirit is not only a blessing to me and our children, but is also precious in God's sight (1 Pet 3:4);

To our four children: Thomas, Annabelle, Elliott, and Augustin—our gifts from God, our reward from Him (Ps 127:3), who gave parts of their childhood enduring patiently the process of sharing their daddy with a pile of books and a laptop and who eagerly looked forward to the day of completion when daddy can spend more time with them;

And to my in-laws, Wes and Jean Woodard, whose ongoing encouragement and faithful prayers reminded me of why I was doing this work and challenged me to see it through.

"Unless fraternal admonition is again restored, accepted, and used according to the earnest behest of Christ, it is not possible that things might proceed aright and stand well among Christians on earth."

—Balthasar Hubmaier

Contents

Foreword by Paige Patterson / ix
Preface / xi

1 The Contextual Milieu of Balthasar Hubmaier and His Theology / 1
2 Church Discipline and Anthropology / 26
3 Church Discipline and Soteriology / 54
4 Church Discipline and Ecclesiology / 82
5 Conclusion / 116

Bibliography / 129
Index / 143

Foreword

NUMEROUS ARTICLES AND SEVERAL monographs are available on the life and theological contribution of Balthasar Hubmaier, whose ministry was known in Germany, Switzerland, Austria, and Czechoslovakia. Some, because of Hubmaier's failure to embrace the doctrine of pacifism, have considered Hubmaier to be wrongly identified with Anabaptism, while others consider him to be the foremost theologian of the Radical Reformation.

However, any student of the period will agree that, among the Radical Reformers, there was no one as colorful as the well tutored Hubmaier; and few, if any, were as successful in the making of a multitude of converts. While there are aspects of his theological contribution that have been considered, what Simon Goncharenko does in this excellent volume is not only to consider Hubmaier's doctrine of church discipline but also to demonstrate the way in which Hubmaier's doctrine of church discipline was uniquely connected to the ordinances of the church. The present study, *Wounds That Heal*, thus becomes an investigation of major importance.

Goncharenko considers the various influences to which Hubmaier was subjected, such as humanism, scholasticism, and late Medieval Augustinism, in the development of his ultimate doctrine of church discipline. The author also spends some time assessing Hubmaier's doctrine of salvation, especially in comparison to Lutheran and Reformed doctrines. Then he turns the discussion to the way in which Hubmaier developed the doctrine of the "Keys of the Kingdom" and baptism and the Lord's Supper in the application of church discipline.

In the contemporary field of monographs on church discipline, the authors of such books are bound to experience a certain measure of frustration since for the most part their call for the renewal of church discipline seems to go unheeded in the contemporary church. Here Goncharenko's assessment of the work of Balthasar Hubmaier makes such a significant step forward. If church discipline does not begin at the point of a mistake on the part of a member of the fellowship but rather at the time of his baptism into the flock of God, and if, furthermore, the supper, among other things, is understood to be a fellowship feast, then suddenly a doctrine of church discipline that can be easily endorsed and practiced by the church emerges. Hubmaier's unique approach to this has never been fully considered before this monograph.

Simon Goncharenko is uniquely qualified to write this book by virtue not only of his scholarly inquiry but also of his background and experience as a Russian Baptist. He has had opportunity to see church discipline practiced in the persecuted church in Russia as well as in the churches that he has served in America. Blended together with this rich dual background of experience, his study of the Radical Reformation in general and of Balthasar Hubmaier in particular provide the matrix for the considerations in this volume.

If one is looking for an opportunity to establish a significant experience in church discipline, there will be few books any more helpful than Goncharenko's *Wounds That Heal: The Importance of Church Discipline within Balthasar Hubmaier's Theology*. While church historians and theologians will have an active interest in the book, it will also be helpful for pastors and churches. Without reservation, I commend this volume for the consideration of these readers.

Paige Patterson
President
Southwestern Theological Baptist Seminary
Fort Worth, TX

Preface

Having grown up in a Baptist church in the Soviet Union, I was able to see church discipline exercised faithfully and quite effectively on several different occasions. I am sure it helped that in a city of 600,000 people there were only two other likeminded churches, so when a person was under the discipline, it was a known fact and there was no place to run. Did it work every time? Did the church discipline that I witnessed achieve its intended result of bringing the sinner back in repentance into the fold? Not always. But, while I cannot answer these questions in the affirmative, what I can say is that from a biblical perspective the church of my childhood years did what it was supposed to do, leaving the final results between the one in rebellion and his Lord.

Fast forward fifteen years and the picture is quite different. Whether it is the lack of resolve, fear of legal repercussions, or just simple unwillingness to initiate the process of church discipline, both of the U.S. churches where I served on staff failed to keep accountable some of their straying members. Of course, it could be that we just do not know enough about the doctrine of church discipline to practice it effectively.

Rewind some 500 years and meet Balthasar Hubmaier—an Anabaptist Reformer and a contemporary of Martin Luther and Ulrich Zwingli. A little known character today, Hubmaier was well known in the sixteenth century by both the aforementioned Magisterial Reformers and the Catholic Church because he dared to take God's word literally, especially when it pertained to ecclesiology. Central to his doctrine of the church was Hubmaier's understanding of church discipline. In fact, Hubmaier's church discipline was of profound importance to the whole of his theology.

My hope is that as we engage in conversation about the importance of church discipline to the theology of Balthasar Hubmaier, it may help to propel further this doctrine as a whole to the forefront of our attention. I further eagerly anticipate that a renewed interest in the doctrine of church discipline in the academy might result in its renaissance in the church. Such is my prayer.

As for the efforts which resulted in the work before you, words seem completely inadequate to express my gratitude to my Lord and Savior Jesus Christ for not only saving me but also entrusting me with the responsibility of learning and communicating the truths contained in his Word and in the works of his faithful servants, and enabling me to carry this work to its completion.

Perhaps I never fully appreciated the sacrifices made by my family until the 2010 Thanksgiving dinner, at which each, in sharing those things for which they were thankful, included daddy's school and dissertation. So I am very thankful for and to my wife Alice and our four children, Thomas, Annabelle, Elliott, and Augustin for sharing their husband and father with a computer and a never-ending stack of books for the last eight years of their lives. Without Alice's sacrifices, endurance, and unending encouragement, I could not have made it thus far. I certainly know that without her editorial assistance readers would notice quickly my grammatical deficiencies which are common to non-native English speakers.

A special recognition and appreciation goes to my in-laws, Wes and Jean Woodard. Wes, a brilliant theologian and able practitioner in his own right, often challenged me, always taught me something new, and inadvertently helped to sharpen me biblically and theologically. Wes and Jean's consistent prayer for us, encouragement of us, and substantive assistance through the years sometimes were the only things that kept us in this race.

I am indebted to the family of Madge Dauphin for investing their worldly riches into eternity. If it was not for their funds that resulted in a scholarship for twelve out of sixteen semesters at Southwestern Baptist Theological Seminary, I am certain that I would not be here today. It was through this scholarship, in fact, that the Lord communicated his guidance to us in the first place, some eight years ago, which culminated in this work.

I am grateful for the wisdom and encouragement of my major supervisor, Dr. Malcolm B. Yarnell, III. Since his strict adherence to the president's instruction to stretch me to the uttermost did not kill me, it must have made me a better man and more precise scholar. President Patterson was also a major driving force behind this work. His suggestion that I look more closely at Balthasar Hubmaier resulted in this manuscript. Dr. Patterson's advice, confidence, and forthrightness combined with concrete help spurred me on and kept me on the straight and narrow.

I cannot forget to thank the amazing staff of Roberts Library at Southwestern Baptist Theological Seminary: from Tiffany Norris in the Ministry by Mail area (which is a wonderful blessing for those of us who reside some distance from the main campus), to Helen Dent in the interlibrary loan department, to the Writing Lab staff, thank you all for your help.

There are so many other people who touched our lives over the course of this project, and, as a result of whose love, kindness, and graciousness, we are here today. Among those are Sarah Woodard, Aurilia and Keith McDonald, John and Candice Woodard, Sam and Dixie Mayfield, Dr. Bill Jones, Barry Calhoun, Helma Hallmark, Jesse and Amy Easley, Gene and Pam Young, Juanita Barfield, Ruth Ann Dailey, Ken Farris, David McLean, Ron and Ina Graham, the wonderful people of Dorcas Wills Memorial Baptist Church of Trinity, Texas, faculty and staff of Malaysia Baptist Theological Seminary in Penang, Malaysia, and many others, who, moved by the Holy Spirit, gave of themselves in a variety of ways, at times when we could not have made it without them. Last but not least, I wanted to mention the Gideons International, which was the vehicle by which the Lord providentially brought me to this country almost twenty years ago, in the summer of 1991.

Simon V. Goncharenko
Midway, TX
2011

1

The Contextual Milieu of Balthasar Hubmaier and His Theology

INTRODUCTION

"UNLESS FRATERNAL ADMONITION IS again restored, accepted, and used according to the earnest behest of Christ, it is not possible that things might proceed aright and stand well among Christians on earth."[1] Penned a little less than five hundred years ago, this statement reflects the significance that the doctrine of church discipline—divided between brotherly admonition and excommunication or ban—played in the theology of one of the greatest voices of the sixteenth-century European Reformation, a prolific writer and the foremost leader of the Anabaptist wing, Balthasar Hubmaier. Living at a time of many changes and much duress in the ecclesiological sphere for someone of his convictions, Hubmaier saw moral laxity as the "besetting weakness of Protestantism."[2] As a relatively new movement, born as a response to and in the midst of the doctrinal and ethical corruption of the Catholic Church, Protestantism, in the eyes of the Radical Reformer, would only be successful if it were committed ardently to practice church discipline.

---

1. Hubmaier, "Admonition," 375; Hubmaier, "Schriften," 339.
2. McDill, "Human Free Will in Hubmaier," 199.

Ministering in the historical setting in which the pressures, persecutions, and imminent dangers forced him to be more of a practitioner-theologian, Hubmaier's attention centered on ecclesiology, the doctrine of the church. And perhaps one of the most important aspects of the church, the one that ensured its purity and survival, was teaching and practicing the discipline. In order fully to appreciate Hubmaier's thinking on church discipline, however, it is essential to examine its convergence with the other doctrines of this Radical, namely, his anthropology, soteriology, and ecclesiology.

It was the pen of Balthasar Hubmaier that produced the earliest Anabaptist programmatic writings, published less than six months after the first adult baptisms in Zurich.[3] As one of the most prominent figures in the Radical movement and the only professional theologian of the Anabaptist Reformation, Hubmaier placed church discipline at the very center of his theological edifice. The reformer's doctrine of church discipline was remarkable in its interrelatedness with the ordinances, the keys of the kingdom, and many, if not most, other areas of theology. As such, a careful and thorough investigation of the Waldshut preacher's theology of church discipline is in order.

In the process of this assessment, the goal of this book is to demonstrate that, central in the theology of Balthasar Hubmaier, the doctrine of church discipline was closely interrelated with his doctrines of anthropology, soteriology (including justification and sanctification), and ecclesiology, particularly the ordinances as the keys of the kingdom.

In light of the renewed interest of the past few decades in the Anabaptist Reformation in general, and one of its leading voices, Balthasar Hubmaier, in particular, prolific research has been dedicated to this area. Perhaps the most important and one of the more recently published manuscripts covering the time period under consideration is *The Radical Reformation* (currently in its third edition) by Harvard historian George Huntston Williams. Williams's own unitarian commitment notwithstanding, the comprehensive nature of his research is what makes his work, in Paige Patterson's words, "the *magnum opus* of all time on the Radical Reformation."[4] Among other more recent works in the field of Hubmaier studies is John Rempel's book examining the Christology of the

---

3. Snyder, "Swiss Anabaptism," 70.
4. Patterson, personal email (24th August, 2010).

Waldshut reformer, entitled *The Lord's Supper in Anabaptism*, published in 1993. Eddie Mabry's widely quoted dissertation entitled "The Baptismal Theology of Balthasar Hubmaier" (1982) was self-published in 1994 under the title *Balthasar Hubmaier's Doctrine of the Church*. In 1983 Peder Martin Idsoe Liland, in an effort to emphasize Hubmaier's import for the Anabaptist Reformation, penned a dissertation under the title "Anabaptist Separatism: A Historical and Theological Study of the Contribution of Balthasar Hubmaier." A more general, yet fairly comprehensive approach to the world of the Anabaptist leader is a dissertation by Emir Caner, completed in 1999, under the title "The Truth Is Unkillable: The Life and Writings of Balthasar Hubmaier, Theologian of Anabaptism." Michael McDill, in his dissertation entitled, "The Centrality of the Doctrine of Human Free Will in the Theology of Balthasar Hubmaier," written in 2001, concentrates on the reformer's unique understanding of the human free will and argues that this understanding forms the core of Hubmaier's theology. Two years later, in 2003, Brian Brewer underscored the indispensability of the union between Hubmaier's view of the sacraments and his doctrine of grace in a dissertation entitled "A Response to Grace: The Sacramental Theology of Balthasar Hubmaier." In 2005 Kirk MacGregor examined the import and implications of the Waldshut reformer's sacramental theology to his doctrine of ecclesiology in a dissertation entitled "The Sacramental Theology of Balthasar Hubmaier and Its Implications for Ecclesiology." It was self-published the following year under the title *A Central European Synthesis of Radical and Magisterial Reform*. Also in 2005, Darren Williamson's research concerning the effect of humanism upon Anabaptism, particularly from the writings of Desiderius Erasmus, appeared in a dissertation entitled "Erasmus of Rotterdam's Influence upon Anabaptism: The Case of Balthasar Hubmaier." In 2008 Antonia Lučic Gonzalez wrote a dissertation dealing with the influence of the early church fathers upon the formation of the Radical Reformer's theological outlook. Its title is "Balthasar Hubmaier and Early Christian Tradition." That same year, in a dissertation entitled "The Shaping of the Two Earliest Anabaptist Catechisms," Jason Graffagnino examined a theological convergence between Hubmaier's *Lehrtafel* (1526/27) and the *Kinderfragen* by the *Unitas Fratrum*.[5] The impetus for this claim came from the geographical proximity of the location from which Hubmaier's catechism

---

5. Indigenous Czech religious minority.

was written to that of the area influenced by the *Unitas Fratrum*.[6] Graffagnino's research comes as an update and an improvement to Jarold Knox Zeman's 1969 manuscript entitled *The Anabaptists and the Czech Brethren in Moravia 1526–1628*.[7]

Considering the vast amount of research dealing with Hubmaier's thought and theology already available, only a portion of which has been listed above, what new contribution does this book intend to make to the present field? To answer this question, some background to the current research may be appropriate. Intrigued by the distinctiveness of Hubmaier's theology of church discipline, I began to read both Hubmaier's own writings and the attempts to decipher the reformer's theology made in the secondary literature. As a result, two noteworthy discoveries were made. First, as a practitioner-theologian whose main focus, "in the heat of controversy and amidst the fires of persecution,"[8] was in the area of ecclesiology, Hubmaier's doctrine of church discipline was extremely important, if not essential, to his theology as a whole. The discussion of the brotherly admonition and the ban, consequently, emerges in at least half of his over thirty treatises written for different occasions. Second, as the doctrine that was absolutely integral to the reformer's general theology, church discipline has its tentacles in almost every other area of theology. Commenting on Anabaptist ecclesiology in general, Erland Waltner's conclusion is applicable to the present focus on the theology of one of the main leaders of Anabaptism, "To be properly understood, . . . Anabaptist ecclesiology must be studied in the light of its entire historical and theological context."[9] Though much research has already been dedicated to Balthasar Hubmaier and his doctrine of church discipline, to this day no thorough examination exists on the interrelatedness between the reformer's doctrine of church discipline and the other major areas of his theology.

The above-mentioned volume of Eddie Mabry's, for example, gives a thorough survey of Hubmaier's ecclesiology in general but fails to

---

6. Among some of the earlier works on the subject of the Radical Reformation, the following are of considerable import: Burrage, *A History*; Newman, *Hubmaier*; Newman, *Church History*; Bax, *Anabaptists*; Pike, *Anabaptists*; Zeman, *Anabaptists and the Czech Brethren*; Vedder, *Hübmaier*.

7. Zeman, *Anabaptists and the Czech Brethren*.

8. Waltner, "Anabaptist Conception," 6.

9. Ibid., 7.

recognize the central nature of reformer's doctrine of church discipline or identify its interrelatedness with the other major theological categories in his work. The same oversight can be detected in MacGregor's work. While his research contributes greatly to an understanding of Hubmaier's doctrine of church discipline, MacGregor's main concern was to examine the link between the reformer's church discipline and the sacraments, within the context of the literal influence of Bernard of Clairvaux.[10] As such, no mention is made within MacGregor's work of the primacy of the doctrine of church discipline or of its convergence with the other doctrines in Hubmaier's writings. Likewise, Liland's dissertation, while conducting a comprehensive examination in the theology of the Waldshut reformer, falls short of giving much, if any, attention to his doctrine of church discipline, saying nothing of its convergence with other doctrines.[11]

To grasp accurately and fully the centrality of Hubmaier's doctrine of church discipline, therefore, more comprehensive research is required, especially focusing on its convergence with such doctrines as anthropology, soteriology, and ecclesiology. In other words, since Hubmaier's doctrine of church discipline has not been properly reviewed, the time has come to integrate the fruit of previous research on this reformer's theology with his understanding of church discipline. This will be the focus of the present work.

HISTORIC CONTEXT

In order to understand better both Balthasar Hubmaier and his world, it is essential to begin this section with some basic definitions, to continue with a short biographical outline, and to conclude with a brief survey of the impact of a number of men whose lives and theological moorings intersected with the Radical Reformer.

Contextual Taxonomy

It may be of value at this point to secure definitions of the most commonly used terms for the purposes of this book.[12] The first such term is

10. MacGregor, *European Synthesis*, 18–22.
11. Liland, "Anabaptist Separatism," 131–40.
12. The following definitions are adopted in consultation with MacGregor, *European Synthesis*, and Williams, *The Radical Reformation*.

"Anabaptist." Kirk R. MacGregor offers one of the best and yet simplest definitions for this term, limiting it to the practitioners of adult baptism who, denying the existence of sacraments (ceremonial mediators of grace), held that baptism and communion were ordained acts of obedience to Christ.

The second term that requires explanation is "Radicals." George Huntston Williams in his massive tome *The Radical Reformation* dubbed those reformers who propagated re-baptism "Radicals," from the Latin *radix* (root), because they attempted to return to the root of New Testament Christianity. Their assumption was that most of what happened in the church between AD 325 and 1525 was in error.[13] Therefore, Radicals in this volume will refer to those individuals or communities administering the New Testament *radix*, or root, of adult baptism.

Finally, the term "Magisterial" may need to be clearly deciphered here. This adjective refers, in the present work, to a top-down approach to religious reform through allegiance to magistrates.

Biographical Outline

Hubmaier was born in the early to mid-1480s in the small Bavarian town of Friedburg, outside Augsburg.[14] Few details can be gathered as to Hubmaier's early life. His parents must have had sufficient means to secure a place for him at the cathedral school of Augsburg where he began his early education. On May 1, 1503, he was matriculated as a clerical student at the University of Freiburg and, upon the completion of the basic course of study, enrolled in theology under Johannes Eck (1483–1543), who later became famous as the opponent of Luther at the Leipzig disputation in 1519, and as a participant in the ill-fated colloquy between Protestants and Roman Catholics held at Regensburg in 1541. With the exception of a few months in 1507, which he spent earning a much-needed income as a teacher in Schaffhausen, Hubmaier resided in Freiburg for almost nine years.

---

13. Klaassen, *Anabaptism*, 9.

14. One of the most detailed biographies of Hubmaier may be found in John Allen Moore's book *Anabaptist Portraits*. This section is compiled in consultation with it, as well as Williamson, "Erasmus & Hubmaier," 26–35; Bergsten, *Hubmaier*; Newman, *Hubmaier*; Vedder, *Hübmaier*; Steinmetz, "Nominalist Motifs in Hubmaier"; Rothkegel, "Anabaptism in Moravia and Silesia"; Zeman, *Anabaptists and the Czech Brethren*, 123–32.

In 1512, he followed Eck to the University of Ingolstadt, where he was awarded a doctorate in theology and was appointed professor. It is probable that next to Eck he was the most accomplished man in the university, the pro-rector of which he became in 1515. While in Ingolstadt, Hubmaier also preached at the Church of St. Mary.

After four years in Ingolstadt, Hubmaier relocated to Regensburg, where he accepted the prestigious position of cathedral preacher.[15] In Regensburg, Hubmaier joined the longstanding anti-Jewish movement, which with his assistance was responsible for driving the majority of the Jewish community out of the city. Debts to Jews were erased and the demolished synagogue was replaced with the new Chapel of the Beautiful Mary. In the process of demolition, a master mason, buried in the ruins, supposed to have been fatally injured, appeared the next day on the streets little the worse for his experience. His escape from death was regarded as miraculous and was attributed to the Virgin Mary. Having been rushed to completion, the church became a resort for pilgrims, and multitudes thought themselves healed or greatly benefited by the Virgin's beneficence exercised in connection with the shrine because of her satisfaction with the expulsion of the Jews and the conversion of the synagogue into a place of Christian devotion. The widely publicized miracles taking place in the chapel brought in pilgrims from all over Germany, encouraged by Hubmaier's passionate sermons extolling the shrine's spiritual benefits. In 1520, at the peak of the pilgrimages, Hubmaier's fame had reached its zenith, making him a well-known figure throughout the southern regions of the Holy Roman Empire and resulting in the influx of some one hundred thousand pilgrims that year alone.

For reasons that are not completely clear, in 1521, Hubmaier abruptly ended his popular and profitable tenure at the Chapel of the Beautiful Mary to take a preaching position at the Church of St. Mary in the tiny provincial town of Waldshut[16] on the frontier lands of Habsburg Austria. It was in Waldshut, between 1521 and 1523, that Hubmaier underwent a transformation from a popular parish priest into a respected evangelical reformer, influenced in part by the Pauline epistles and the writings of Martin Luther. Hubmaier briefly resumed his previous position in Regensburg in the late fall of 1522 without resigning from Waldshut,

---

15. *Domprediger.*
16. The town population was around 1,000 people.

but after only a few months he returned to Waldshut. It is believed that one of the reasons for the brevity of the second stay in Regensburg was Hubmaier's capitulation to the Lutheran reformation, a transformation which took place in the winter of 1522.

Back in Waldshut, the proximity to Zurich ended up playing an important role in Hubmaier's theological pilgrimage, as the theology of its main reformer, Ulrich Zwingli, proved to be far more decisive to Hubmaier than the theology of Luther. In 1523, the Waldshut preacher boldly aligned himself with Zwingli's reformation in Zurich when he participated in the October disputation. His convergence with Zwingli's theology ended by early 1525 as Hubmaier rejected infant baptism and began moving toward Anabaptism.

On the Saturday before Easter Sunday (15 April) in 1525, he was re-baptized by Wilhelm Reublin, along with some sixty of his associates, and later baptized more than three hundred of his parishioners in Waldshut using a milk pail. As Anabaptist reform in Waldshut coincided with the German Peasants' War, Hubmaier and the town council supported and aided the peasant cause, a move which later that year cost him his position. As Habsburg troops occupied Waldshut in December of 1525, Hubmaier and his wife, Elsbeth Hugeline, whom he had married the previous January, were on the run. Zurich ended up being their next destination, as they were deterred from every other direction by Austrian troops. Four traumatic months later, which included incarceration, torture authorized by Zwingli, and recantation from his Anabaptist views, a lapse he later bitterly regretted, Hubmaier and his wife departed Zurich.

His initial escape was to Augsburg, where, in May of 1526, Hubmaier baptized John Denck.[17] Three months later, however, in July of 1526, Hubmaier arrived in the Moravian town of Nikolsburg (Mikulov),[18] a

---

17. Elsewhere referred to as Hansk Denck, he was an evangelical Spiritualist influenced by Müntzer, who believed that the seeming paradoxes of Scripture could be resolved by the harmonizing operation of the Holy Spirit bringing together the disparate scriptural words in the reader's dynamic encounter with the inner Word called forth by the eternal Logos.

18. The town is situated along the trade route from Brünn (Brno) to Vienna at the southern end of the Pollau Hills, a highly visible landmark not far from the Lower Austrian border. The domain of Nikolsburg, populated by German-speaking Catholics, had been a possession of the Lords of Liechtenstein since the middle of the thirteenth century. By the time of Hubmaier's arrival, the population of the city numbered between 2500 and 3000 people.

region that was more tolerant of religious dissent, and, as such, attracted a large number of Anabaptists. Within a few months, Hubmaier's skill and charisma helped to create in the city a thriving Anabaptist movement of more than two thousand, including the protector himself, Prince Leonhard von Liechtenstein, the group of which Hubmaier himself became the leader. Hubmaier's literary activity in Nikolsburg was very fruitful, where, in less than a year, he published no fewer than fifteen distinct treatises, some of which were written before he left Waldshut.

The commotion caused in part by the wide distribution of his writings and in part by the millennarian and communist views propagated by the likes of John Hut,[19] Jacob Wiedemann, and Philip Jäger,[20] attracted the attention of King Ferdinand of Austria. The Liechtensteins were unable to protect their great leader and his wife who were arrested for his alleged seditious activity dating to the Peasants' War. Transported to Kreuzenstein castle near Vienna for interrogation in 1527, Hubmaier, this time steadfast under torture, was eventually condemned as a rebellious heretic and burned at the stake in Vienna on March 10, 1528. Three days later, his wife, whose loyalty to her husband and his principles had never wavered, was also condemned and shared his fate, only by drowning in the Danube.

19. Elsewhere referred to as Hans Hut, he was one of the disciples of Thomas Müntzer, a book peddler, who in 1524 had seen to the publication in Nuremberg of Müntzer's most important pamphlet, the *Manifest Exposé of False Faith*. Becoming the most successful Anabaptist missionary in South Germany and Austria, in 1526 and 1527, and elaborating many themes of Müntzer's message, Hut also went beyond anything Müntzer had ever said or written, proclaiming that the world would end in 1528. Hut declared that at this apocalyptic moment the elect of God would be permitted to draw the sword of vengeance, which was to remain in its sheath until then. His arrival in Nikolsburg completed the polarization of the refugee community in that he placed in an intensely eschatological framework the expendable role of the magistrate-patron and their own preeminance of the agapetic communism in imitation of the Pentecostal community of goods in Acts. Hut was one of the major opponents of Hubmaier at the Nikolsburg Disputation of 1527, where the main points of contention were regarding the use of the sword, the propriety of paying taxes for military purposes in defense of Christendom, and the role of a benevolent and even regenerate magistracy with respect to the role of the sword at Christ's second advent.

20. Pacifist radical Separatists, one-eyed Swabian, Wiedemann, and Jäger go down in Hutterite tradition as the *Stäbler* (Anabaptists of the staff in place of the sword). It was Wiedemann and Jäger who organized the Nicolsburg Disputation. Their group practiced full community of goods and elected two stewards to manage the temporal needs of the believers.

In Moore's apt description, Hubmaier was "a person who would seek doggedly for the truth, according to the light available to him at the time."[21] At the end, it was the Word of God that captured his mind and heart as the only way that seemed right to this Radical Reformer and he "felt impelled to give his all to it."[22] Devoted to Scripture alone, Hubmaier was known to restate the notion that in case of error he was willing to be corrected out of God's Word and that, due to this desire, he could not be a heretic.[23] It was this very allegiance to the Word of God, which he could not and would not shake, that cost him his life.

Early Influences

From its very inception, Anabaptism as a movement was diverse, multi-faceted, and variegated. Perhaps one of the best characterizations of Anabaptism and its contribution to the modern Christian culture comes from the pen of Rufus M. Jones:

> Judged by the reception it met at the hands of those in power, both in Church and State, equally in Roman Catholic and in Protestant countries, the Anabaptist movement was one of the most tragic in the history of Christianity; but, judged by the principles, which were put into play by the men who bore this reproachful nickname, it must be pronounced one of the most momentous and significant undertakings in man's eventful religious struggle after the truth. It gathered up the gains of earlier movements, it is the spiritual soil out of which all nonconformist sects have sprung, and it is the first plain announcement in modern history of a programme for a new type of Christian society which the modern world, especially in America and England, has been slowly realizing—an absolutely free and independent religious society, and a State in which every man counts as a man, and has his share in shaping both Church and State.[24]

Many attempts have been made in the past to reduce to one basic idea all the divergent and often mutually exclusive opinions that characterized

---

21. Moore, *Anabaptist Portraits*, 172.

22. John Allen Moore, *Anabaptist Portraits*, 172.

23. Hubmaier, "An Earnest Christian Ayt6ppeal to Schaffhausen," 46; Hubmaier, "Schriften," 83.

24. Jones, *Studies in Mystical Religion*, 369.

Anabaptism, but these are to be regarded only as a misleading oversimplification of historical facts.[25]

Made up of people who were "dissatisfied with the often indecisive and cautious progress of the Reformation and wanted more radical reform recklessly challenging the ecclesiastical and secular authorities,"[26] Anabaptism was known for its critique of infant baptism and the practice of a baptism of faith and confession, which was the source of its derogatory label, "Anabaptists."[27] The majority of the adherents of the Anabaptist movement gladly welcomed Luther's call to *sola fide* and *sola scriptura* and Zwingli's commemorative understanding of the sacraments, all the while wondering why the implications of their declarations were not nurtured and developed by the reformers themselves.[28] As such, retaining the original vision of Luther and Zwingli, the Anabaptists, in the words of Harold S. Bender, "enlarged it, gave it body and form, and set out to achieve it in actual experience."[29] For, in the eyes of many Anabaptists, "just as personal faith was essential to salvation, a disciplined church was essential to witness."[30] The radicalism of the Radical Reformers, therefore, was mainly limited to the area of the ecclesiological implications of the tenets of the Magisterial Reformation. For, when it came to soteriological concerns, the Radical Reformers were not radical enough from the perspective of Luther and Calvin.[31]

As to their accomplishments, they were the first to practice the complete separation of church and state. Their sectarianism, particularly their refusal, on the basis of the Sermon on the Mount, to swear oaths and to undertake any form of military service, was deemed to undermine two foundations of contemporaneous political life. This was considered an expression of hostility to ordered society and it resulted in ruthless persecution.[32]

25. Zeman, *Anabaptists and the Czech Brethren*, 31.
26. Jürgen-Goertz, *Anabaptists*, 7.
27. "Täufer" or "Wiedertäufer", which mean re-baptizers. "This title," according to Walker, Norris, Lotz, and Handy, "was both inaccurate and prejudicial, since they recognized but one baptism, that for adults only, and so denied the validity of their baptisms in infancy." See Walker, et al., *Christian Church*, 449.
28. Patterson, "Learning from the Anabaptists," 124.
29. Bender, "Anabaptist Vision," 41.
30. Patterson, "Learning from the Anabaptists," 125.
31. Steinmetz, *Reformers in the Wings*, 145.
32. Walker, et al., *Christian Church*, 449.

While understood by most to be a participant in the Anabaptist branch of the sixteenth-century European reformation, Balthasar Hubmaier, in the words of Darren T. Williamson, "was a capable and creative theologian who did not easily fit into one theological mold."[33] Hubmaier's theology was so unique, and in some areas so unlike the theological moorings of either the Magisterial or Anabaptist reformers that the time may have come for a thorough re-classification of his theology. For the purpose of the current research, however, Hans Jürgen-Goertz's summation of the Waldshut reformer's theological position as "retaining something of Protestant character," while at the same time displaying "traces of Catholic theology and piety," will suffice.[34]

As no theology is developed in a vacuum, it is important to one's understanding of Balthasar Hubmaier and his unique positions to be informed of the theological landscape of sixteenth-century Europe in which the Radical Reformer operated. This landscape consisted of various adherents to the Roman Catholic and early Protestant branches of Christianity. Among these are such men as Johannes Eck, Desiderius Erasmus, Martin Luther, and Ulrich Zwingli.[35]

Eck

Johannes Eck was one of the Radical Reformer's early Catholic teachers. As Hubmaier's professor at the University of Freiburg and a man of great import in the context of the sixteenth-century European Reformation, Eck acquired a powerful influence over the young theologian and encouraged him in his rapid progress in theology.[36] According to David C. Steinmetz, Eck himself was "strongly influenced in his theology by the nominalism of Gabriel Biel, especially in his view of justification."[37]

---

33. Williamson, "Erasmus & Hubmaier," 224.

34. Jürgen-Goertz, *Anabaptists*, 6.

35. While in his theological studies Hubmaier was exposed not only to the theology of Duns Scotus and Thomas Aquinas, but also to such modern theologians as William Occam, Gabriel Biel, Robert Holkot and John Major of Haddington, a commitment to maintaining a proper focus on the present research necessitates that this section be limited to a survey of the major influences in the life and theological pilgrimage of the Radical Reformer. For a more detailed listing of the theologians that impacted the Waldshut Reformer, please see the sources in note 27, the first part of chapter 2, and Steinmetz, "Nominalist Motifs in Hubmaier."

36. Williams, *The Radical Reformation*, 149.

37. Steinmetz, *Reformers in the Wings*, 139.

The Contextual Milieu of Balthasar Hubmaier and His Theology 13

Walter L. Moore argues that the common theological ground between Hubmaier and Eck was quite extensive, and that there is no evidence that the former, for all of his theological movement, ever left it.[38] As part of this common ground, argues Steinmetz, Eck transferred his Nominalist leanings to his disciple.[39] Like the Nominalists, Hubmaier assumed a binding covenant between God and man and distinguished between the absolute and the ordained power of God.[40] It was partly due to Eck's influence on Hubmaier, furthermore, that the latter became interested in Christian Humanism and particularly its greatest proponent of the sixteenth century, Catholic reformer Desiderius Erasmus.

Erasmus

The theme of Erasmian influence on the early Swiss Anabaptist movement was taken up in some detail in the last century resulting in a number of different positions. Some, like Robert Kreider, believe that Humanism in general had a "profound influence on the rise of the Anabaptist movement," if not in specific ideas and doctrines, then at least in methods and attitudes.[41] Others suggest that the Anabaptists were dependent upon Erasmus for their views on freedom of the will,[42] their pacifism,[43] and their ethical sincerity.[44]

Abraham Friesen, Professor Emeritus of Renaissance and Reformation history at the University of California, Santa Barbara, in his volume entitled *Erasmus, the Anabaptists and the Great Commission*, takes the previous claims for the Anabaptists' dependence on Erasmus a step further by forging a thought-provoking argument attributing the birth of Anabaptism to the prince of Humanists. Friesen's assertion, assuming a monogenesis theory of Anabaptist beginnings,[45] traces the pro-

---

38. Walter L. Moore, Jr., "Eck & Hubmaier," 68–97.

39. Steinmetz, "Nominalist Motifs in Hubmaier."

40. Steinmetz, *Reformers in the Wings*, 143; Walter L. Moore, Jr., "Eck & Hubmaier," 85; Hubmaier, "Freedom of the Will, II," 472; Hubmaier, "Schriften," 416.

41. Kreider, "Anabaptism and Humanism," 140.

42. Hall, "Erasmian Influence."

43. Fast, "First Anabaptists & Luther, Erasmus, and Zwingli."

44. Kenneth Davis, "Erasmus as a Progenitor of Anabaptist Theology and Piety."

45. The monogenesis (single origin) theory of Anabaptist origins, introduced in 1943 by Harold Bender to the American Society of Church History through his presidential address entitled "The Anabaptist Vision," Bender, "Anabaptist Vision," 33, was a response

found impact of Erasmus' discussion of the Matthean version of the Great Commission and its relation to the baptismal passages in Acts upon both the origin and the development of Anabaptist thought. With baptism, for example, it was Erasmus' Neoplatonic perspective that allowed him to hold the ideal[46] and the real[47] together in considerable tension rather than breaking with the Catholic Church altogether. Thus, what the Catholic Humanist elucidated in his 1516, 1519, and 1522 editions of the New Testament and the various editions of his *Annotations* that accompanied them, were the central thoughts and ideas that would be championed later by the Anabaptists. "Were one to read Erasmus without his Neoplatonic perspective," adds Friesen, "one might nearly think him an Anabaptist.[48]

That Erasmus had an influence of consequence upon the Anabaptist movement in general has been a majority view for some time. Similarly, the aforementioned theologians[49] holding the majority view are also of the opinion that the great Humanist shaped in part the theology of Hubmaier. They support such assertions by mentioning, first, Hubmaier's short visit with Erasmus in Basel in 1522.[50] Second, they point to the inclusion of

to the earlier simplistic (and incorrect) linkage of *all* Anabaptists with Thomas Müntzer and the Münsterites. The adherents of this theory argued that a single Anabaptist succession, which spread throughout central and northern Europe at the hands of prominent leaders like Pilgram Marpeck, Peter Riedeman, and Menno Simons, was conceived at the Second Zurich Disputation in October 1523. The monogenesis theory was later countered by the polygenesis theory (multiple origins), which claimed that Anabaptism was not a single movement with a consistent common theological core, but rather was a movement in progress, evolving only gradually from an initial popular mass church concept (*Volkskirche*) to a separatist Free Church (*Freikirche*) in the context of the Peasants War, and can consequentially only be understood chronologically and historically (Reimer, "Recent Anabaptist Studies," 236). The polygenetic interpretive model described Anabaptism as composed of three movements with distinctly individual origins: the Swiss, the South German/Austrian, and the North German/Dutch, Snyder, "Beyond Polygenesis," 6.

46. Taking his cue from the monastic movement's idea of the monastic initiation as a second baptism, Erasmus came extremely close to advocating rebaptism as a ceremony during which a person would take for himself the baptismal vow that was applied to him in infancy.

47. The situation described by Erasmus in which most of his contemporaries had no idea what vows they undertook in the baptism ceremony.

48. Friesen, *Erasmus*, 36.

49. To their number can be added Bergsten, *Hubmaier*, 444; Armour, *Anabaptist Baptism*, 24–27; Steinmetz, "Nominalist Motifs in Hubmaier," 137–44; Williams, *The Radical Reformation*, 156; Mabry, *Doctrine of the Church*, 26–30.

50. In Basel, Hubmaier discussed the doctrine of purgatory with Erasmus and the

Erasmus' baptismal theology in the Radical's *Old and New Believers on Baptism*. Here Hubmaier synthesized Erasmus' teachings on baptism, as recorded in the latter's 1523 paraphrase of the Gospel of Matthew:

> He [Erasmus] recounts all the articles of faith as they are contained in the *Symbolo Apostolorum*, [The Apostles' Creed] and adds these words: "After you have taught the people these things and they believe what you have taught them, have repented of their prior life, and are ready henceforth to walk according to evangelical doctrine, then immerse them in water in the name of the Father and the Son and the Holy Spirit." Here Erasmus publicly points out that baptism was instituted by Christ for those instructed in faith and not for young children.[51]

Hubmaier then turned from Erasmus' paraphrase of Christ's Great Commission to his paraphrase of the Acts of the Apostles, stating: "He [Erasmus] writes further on the second chapter of Acts (2:38): 'The Lord commanded the evangelical shepherds: Go forth and teach all peoples, baptize them, teach them to hold all things which I have commanded you,' Matt. 28:19. Teach those who are to be baptized the basic elements of evangelical wisdom. Unless one believes the same, then he is immersed in water in vain. Consider him also, dear reader, on the eighth chapter of Acts and many other places."[52]

As one who "wrote with constraint,"[53] Erasmus never opposed infant baptism in his *Paraphrases on the New Testament*, or anywhere else, yet spending time with the Humanist in person must have given Hubmaier the impetus to interpret the former's affirmation of pre-baptismal instruction as an implicit denial of the practice.[54]

In his other citations of Erasmus, Hubmaier continues along the same vein. In the *Dialogue with Zwingli's Baptism Book*, the Radical discredits infant baptism by arguing that the trinitarian formula used

---

exegesis of John 1:13, where the conversation most likely revolved around the question of free will. Noting a discrepancy between what Erasmus taught personally and what he was willing to put in writing, Hubmaier expressed some antipathy toward Erasmus' character, recollecting his visit in a letter to a friend with the following words: *Libere loquitur Erasmus, sed anguste scribit* ("Erasmus speaks freely, but writes with constraint"), but did not express antipathy toward what Erasmus taught.

51. Hubmaier, "Old & New Teachers," 255; Hubmaier, "Schriften," 233.
52. Hubmaier, "Old & New Teachers," 255–56; Hubmaier, "Schriften," 233.
53. See note 43.
54. Williamson, "Erasmus & Hubmaier," 60.

in its administration derives from Matthew 28:19, yet "these words still do not apply to young children, also according to the understanding of Jerome, Erasmus, and Zwingli, yea the old and new teachers."[55] Two years later, in the *Dialogue with Oecolampad on Infant Baptism*, the Waldshut reformer reiterates the same themes and cites Erasmus once again. Pointing to the fact that Christ blessed, loved, and embraced children prior to their baptism, Hubmaier asks: "Then what need do they have of baptism, since the general institution of water baptism does not apply to them also, according to the understanding of Origen, Basil the Great, Athanasius, Tertullian, Jerome, Erasmus, and Zwingli? I want to let their books be my witnesses."[56] Finally, those who hold to Erasmian influence upon Hubmaier add to their evidence the latter's extensive use of the former's *On the Freedom of the Will* in his own treatise of the same title. Although they recognize that Hubmaier never explicitly referred to Erasmus' work, these same scholars are fairly certain that the Radical Reformer was deeply indebted to the Humanist, "despite some variations from Erasmus' argument."[57]

Opposing the majority view are theologians like Kirk R. MacGregor[58] and Walter L. Moore,[59] who assert that it was Erasmus who was influenced by Hubmaier. Moore suggests that, while Hubmaier composed *Freedom of the Will* toward the end of his ministry, the viewpoint defended in this tract constitutes the same position held by the reformer throughout his whole life. To this MacGregor adds the evidence of a 1521 letter to the Humanist John Sapidus which affirms the constancy of Hubmaier's anthropology and helps to refute the notion that he altered his previously Lutheran-Zwinglian views upon reading Erasmus' *De libero arbitrio*.[60] This is because the Sapidus letter antedates by three years Erasmus' 1524 *Diatribe*.

All in all, however, whether Erasmus influenced Hubmaier or vice versa is not as consequential for the purposes of this book as is illustrating the existence of a convergence between the paths of the Catholic and

---

55. Ibid., 60; Hubmaier, "Dialogue," 227; Hubmaier, "Schriften," 209.

56. Hubmaier, "On Infant Baptism," 291–92; Hubmaier, "Schriften," 267.

57. Williamson, "Erasmus & Hubmaier," 61; Hall, "Erasmian Influence"; Bergsten, *Hubmaier*, 352–58.

58. MacGregor, *European Synthesis*, 38–40.

59. Walter L. Moore, Jr., "Eck & Hubmaier," 95.

60. MacGregor, *European Synthesis*, 39.

The Contextual Milieu of Balthasar Hubmaier and His Theology 17

Radical Reformers. While these questions may be up for debate, the fact that contact was established between the two, whether through their meeting in Basel or through Hubmaier's inclusion of Erasmus by name in at least three of his treatises, is beyond contestation, which is precisely what this research set out to illustrate.

Summarizing Hubmaier's development as of June of 1522, Windhorst concludes, "it is evident that he was strongly influenced by humanism, turning towards the study of the Pauline letters, and also facing the Reformation desires of Luther with an open mind, all the while on the outside carrying out the duties of a Roman priest."[61] Windhorst makes a very important point here in establishing a connection between the influences of humanism and Hubmaier's successive turn to Scripture. Kenneth Ronald Davis, in his tome *Anabaptism and Asceticism*, makes a similar observation noting that an intersection with humanism encouraged Hubmaier "to intensify his own study of Scripture," which resulted in the recognition of the Bible as "the ultimate norm for all religious reform."[62] At the end, Darren T. Williamson's conclusion regarding Hubmaier's interaction with Erasmus is absolutely accurate when he states that "there can be no question that Hubmaier knew Erasmus' work, appreciated his thought, and admired his method."[63]

Luther

As for the early Protestant influences, the groundwork for the theological landscape was laid out by Magisterial Reformers like Martin Luther and Ulrich Zwingli. The magnitude of Luther's revolutionary contribution to the European Reformation of the sixteenth century cannot be overstated. "For it was Luther," according to Heinold Fast's astute observation, "who not only brought the Reformation to the point of precipitation, but who also produced the ideas lying at its basis."[64] As a result, there is a general sense in which Anabaptism, which followed in time the work of the Magisterial Reformers, was dependent on the Wittenberg reformer.

---

61. "so zeigt sich, daß er vom Humanismus stark beeinflußt war, sich dem Studium der paulinischen Briefe zuwandte, und auch den reformatorischen Anliegen Luthers aufgeschlossen gegenüberstand, während er nach außen hin den Pflichten eines römischen Priesters nachkam." See Windhorst, *Täferisches Taufverständnis*, 10.

62. Kenneth Ronald Davis, *Anabaptism and Asceticism*, 102.

63. Williamson, "Erasmus & Hubmaier," 63.

64. Fast, "First Anabaptists & Luther, Erasmus, and Zwingli," 105.

Moving beyond this general dependence, however, Fast enumerates seven points of convergence between Luther's key pursuits and those of the Anabaptists'.

First, the central concern shared by Luther and the Anabaptists was to call men to repentance, the kind that was not accomplished "by means of single good deeds or works," or by following "an ecclesiastical ceremony of penitence, but by a conversion of the heart."[65] Second, both Luther and the Anabaptists held that only God could accomplish this radical repentance. Repentance is a gift to those willing to "face the wounds of Christ," through whom God has spoken decisively and in whom God's love for humanity is revealed.[66] Third, there was equally high significance given to the Holy Spirit by both Luther and the Anabaptists. Both believed that the Holy Spirit's role in appointing men to the office of preaching the gospel was sufficient enough, thereby abolishing the need for the Roman hierarchical confirmations.[67] Fourth, through Luther the concept of faith deepened to the point where it became entirely personal and affixed. The Anabaptists shared this sense of liberty of conscience with the Wittenberg reformer.[68] Fifth, although the two may not have agreed on the meaning or form of the ordinances, particularly baptism, both Luther and the Anabaptists held to the necessity of faith for the efficacy of the ordinances.[69] Sixth, Luther began and the Anabaptists developed to the fullest, the idea of a church consisting of a smaller limited circle. In Luther's mind it

---

65. Ibid., 105; Muralt and Schmid, *Quellen zur Geschichte*, 40–42. Repentance was one of the underlying themes for Luther's ninety-five theses. It is no surprise, therefore, that in the first statement, which may be considered the title of the whole ninety-five theses, Luther writes, "When our Lord and Master Jesus Christ said, 'Repent' [Matt. 4:17], he willed the entire life of believers to be one of repentance," Luther, *Luther's Works*, 83.

66. Fast, "First Anabaptists & Luther, Erasmus, and Zwingli," 105; Luther, *Luther's Works*, 83.

67. Fast, "First Anabaptists & Luther, Erasmus, and Zwingli," 106. Luther addressed the German nobles with the following words, for example, "Pope, emperor, and universities may make Doctors of Arts, of Medicine, of Laws, of the Sentences; but be assured that no man can make a Doctor of Holy Scripture except the Holy Spirit from heaven," Luther, *Luther's Works*, 205.

68. Fast, "First Anabaptists & Luther, Erasmus, and Zwingli," 107; Luther, *Luther's Works*, 49–59.

69. Fast, "First Anabaptists & Luther, Erasmus, and Zwingli," 107. In *The Babylonian Captivity of the Church*, Luther writes, "it is not baptism that justifies or benefits anyone, but it is faith in that word of promise to which baptism is added," Luther, *Luther's Works*, 66, 73; Luther, *Luther's Works*, 64.

was limited to such as earnestly desired to be Christian, whereas for the Anabaptists, the church consisted of those of age to be taught and properly baptized.[70] Seventh, Fast believes that the Anabaptist distinctive of validating everything by the Scripture can be traced back to Luther, who held the Bible to be "the only norm in all these questions as opposed to all tradition."[71] The aforementioned points of convergence illustrate at least one simple fact well: in the process of reforming Wittenberg, Luther made some general leaps forward in the theological arena of sixteenth-century Europe, leaps which were picked up and enlarged upon by the subsequent generation of Radical Reformers.

The level to which Luther affected the Anabaptist movement as a whole may be debatable; what is not, however, is Luther's influence in the theological pilgrimage of Balthasar Hubmaier, who was directly impacted by the Wittenberg reformer. Hubmaier's first impulse to join the Reformation, in fact, came from the reading of Luther's 1520 *Ein sermon von dem neuen Testament, das ist von der heiligen Messe*, which would henceforth remain his favorite of all Luther's works. Commenting on that, Mabry has suggested that among the "Anabaptists, perhaps no one was more influenced by the writings of Luther than Hubmaier."[72]

The Waldshut reformer was particularly intrigued by Luther's notion of the necessity of personal faith for valid reception of the sacraments and his hermeneutical principle of *sola scriptura* plus faithful reason, both of which Hubmaier adopted. An initial misunderstanding of Luther's concept of "faith," resulting from viewing it through Hubmaier's own tripartite anthropology, caused the latter to conclude that Luther believed that infant baptism was invalid. This notion was further confirmed in Hubmaier's mind when Luther did not respond to his letter of inquiry regarding the subject. "When Hubmaier encountered the complete exposition of Luther's views on faith as a monergistic gift of God and pedobaptism as both proper and valid in *Vom Anbeten des Sacraments des heiligen Leichnams Christi*, however, the Radical's original perception was quickly shattered," according to MacGregor.[73]

---

70. Fast, "First Anabaptists & Luther, Erasmus, and Zwingli," 108.
71. Ibid.
72. Mabry, *Doctrine of the Church*, 32.
73. MacGregor, *European Synthesis*, 128.

Rollin Stely Armour summarized well the pivotal role of Luther in shaping Hubmaier's views: "He himself claimed that the first direct stimulus toward a reexamination of baptism came from Luther, specifically from Luther's . . . *Ein Sermon von dem neuen Testament, das ist von Heiligen Messe*, in which Hubmaier found Luther stressing the importance of faith for the sacraments . . . Although Luther did not intend what Hubmaier attributed to him, it is probably true that Hubmaier's first questions about baptism did arise from Luther's doctrine."[74]

The profundity of Luther's influence in the life of Hubmaier can be seen even in the Anabaptist's later years in Nikolsburg when he was still described, and did not protest such labeling, as a *Lutherische*.

Zwingli

Ulrich Zwingli, the Zurich reformer, is also particularly significant to the field of Hubmaier studies, due to the vast amount of theological interaction he was destined to have with the Anabaptist reformer. Moreover, as mentioned before, those holding to the monogenesis theory of the Anabaptist beginnings would go so far as to assign the credit for the Anabaptist movement to Zwingli's unwillingness to progress in his own theology beyond a certain point. This is evident from the following statement by Heinold Fast, who, in effect, credits the Zurich reformer with the birth of Anabaptism: "previous to the formation of an independent congregation under the sign of adult baptism in Zürich in 1524–25 there was no Anabaptism as such, and the total Anabaptist movement of the following years cannot be imagined without the impetus emanating from the first Swiss Brethren who were expelled from Zürich and continued to be everywhere persecuted."[75] The Anabaptists in Zurich, therefore, "proceeded from a circle of close friends of Zwingli, who supported Zwingli most powerfully in his reform efforts at the beginning of the second decade of the sixteenth century, and were theologically completely dependent upon him."[76]

As to the specific areas in which Anabaptist theology draws its impetus from the doctrinal position of Ulrich Zwingli, Fast enumerates the following three: the preaching of repentance and conversion as a central

74. Armour, *Anabaptist Baptism*, 24.
75. Fast, "First Anabaptists & Luther, Erasmus, and Zwingli," 104.
76. Ibid., 111.

element of the Anabaptist piety;[77] the particular understanding of baptism in which salvation does not depend on water but on faith;[78] and the view of communion as creating and obligating participants to fellowship.[79] Related to communion, what is especially intriguing is that a scrupulous analysis of Grebel's letter to Thomas Müntzer, which happens to be the first comprehensive formulation of the Lord's Supper in the Anabaptist theology, reveals that every point of Grebel's exposition has been taken from Zwingli.[80]

Although it may be impossible to contest Zwingli's key role in the initial development of the Swiss Anabaptist movement as a whole, the same cannot be stated as emphatically with regard to the evolution of Hubmaier's theology. With that being the case, some of the recently presented evidence indicates that when Prior Ruckensperger vom Klaster Sion arranged the first meeting of Zwingli with Hubmaier in Zurich, this rendezvous was between two already established evangelical reformers,[81] rather than the former idea that Zwingli was taking Hubmaier under his wing.[82] The contention of the scholars presenting this evidence is that, for all the interaction that Hubmaier had with Zwingli, he was never considered "Zwinglian" himself. One part of the evidence shows that long before 1524, the point at which infant baptism "first became an issue in the Zurich Reformation, Hubmaier was already refusing to administer the rite, of which he served as a leading opponent since at least 1523, and was baptizing mostly believers from that point forward."[83] Perhaps another reason why caution should be exercised when describing various influences in the life and the theological development of Balthasar Hubmaier or when affixing labels to his views and doctrinal positions is that the Radical Reformer himself never espoused what he considered

---

77. Huldreich Zwingli, *ZW*, 3:142ff, as quoted in Fast, "First Anabaptists & Luther, Erasmus, and Zwingli," 112.

78 . Huldreich Zwingli, *ZW*, 2:2:122ff, as quoted in ibid., 114.

79. Ulrich Zwingli, *Works*, 114–21; as quoted in ibid., 113. See also MacGregor, *European Synthesis*, 7.

80. Muralt and Schmid, *Quellen zur Geschichte*, 13–29; as quoted in Fast, "First Anabaptists & Luther, Erasmus, and Zwingli," 116–19.

81. MacGregor, *European Synthesis*, 119.

82. See for instance Williams, *The Radical Reformation*, 222. Estep, *Anabaptist Story*, 81; Pipkin, "The Baptismal Theology," 34–35.

83. MacGregor, *European Synthesis*, 121.

to be Zwingli's and Luther's views on the bondage of the will, on predestination, and on exclusively forensic justification; and later he openly repudiated them. The subject of justification, within the larger umbrella of Hubmaier's understanding of salvation, will be the focus of chapter 3.

INTRODUCTION TO HUBMAIER'S CONCEPT OF CHURCH DISCIPLINE

Prior to diving into the sea of Hubmaier's doctrine of church discipline and its intersection with the rest of his theology, it is necessary to provide here a short introduction to the subject. To begin, the process of discipline is divided into two steps, namely brotherly admonition, which is outlined in his treatise *On Fraternal Admonition*,[84] and the ban, also known as excommunication, delineated in his *On the Christian Ban*.[85]

Every believer, according to Hubmaier, had agreed and committed to being admonished *de facto* at the point of believers' baptism.[86] The admonishment or discipline exercised by the church stood in direct correlation to the seriousness of one's offense. If the sin committed by the offender belonged to the secret category, a Matthean escalation formula was used, as delineated in chapter 18 of that Gospel: a personal confrontation was followed by the visit from a group of two to three and was concluded, in the event it was unsuccessful, by congregational discipline.[87] Those sins which belonged to the public category were dealt with publicly and immediately. The purpose of Hubmaier's church discipline was fourfold, the first three of which have been documented before: first, to keep the church pure and unpolluted by shame before the outside world; second, to keep believers within the fold from stumbling and joining the offender in sinful pursuits; and third, to cause the offender to repent and eventually be brought back into the fold: "It was better for you that you should be excluded and considered as a pagan, rather than that you would bring to shame the whole church through scandal, and that you might have seduced other members with yourself into sin and eternal perdition. It was also more profitable for you, for the reason that you might come to aware-

---

84. Hubmaier, "Admonition"; Hubmaier, "Schriften".
85. Hubmaier, "Ban"; Hubmaier, "Schriften".
86. Hubmaier, "Ban," 416; Hubmaier, "Schriften," 371.
87. Hubmaier, "Admonition," 377; Hubmaier, "Schriften," 341.

ness, recognize your misery, abstain from sins, and then be received again by the church with great joy and admitted into her Christian fellowship."[88]

The fourth purpose of Hubmaier's doctrine of church discipline, as this work intends to demonstrate, is to serve the rest of his theology as one of the unifying factors and a means by which his theology is grounded into praxis.

Where congregational admonition went unheeded, the ban was exercised. Here it must be noted that, when compared to most of his contemporaries within the Anabaptist movement, Hubmaier's idea of excommunication was much more civil than theirs. His shunning was not to include such extreme actions as striking, banishing, or executing, but was to be limited to avoiding the offender, fleeing from him, and staying out of his company.[89] Furthermore, also unlike the common practice of the ban for most sixteenth-century Radicals, in Hubmaier's church family members of the excommunicated ones were not forced to abstain from every form of communication, including intimate interaction.

The banned members were not to be viewed as enemies but as brothers and were to be reminded from time to time why they were being shunned. Because they were not considered enemies, Hubmaier allowed certain "works of necessity" to be done for them, such as providing those in extreme need with food, drink, and shelter. It was the "works of friendship," meaning normal social interactions, that were not allowed.[90]

What is clearly evident from even a cursory reading of Hubmaier's treatises on church discipline is his concern to be biblically accurate in its exercise. Not only does he offer plentiful biblical support and examples for the subject at hand, but he also remains consistent with the New Testament focus for church discipline, making the restoration of the believer his underlying motive behind the practice of discipline. To that end, he concludes *On the Christian Ban* with instructions for restoration in a section entitled: "How to Deal with the Returning Sinner."[91]

It must also be mentioned here that Hubmaier viewed the subject of church discipline through the lenses of the keys, which the ascended Christ handed to the church to be utilized until his second coming. More

---

88. Hubmaier, "Admonition," 380; Hubmaier, "Schriften," 343.
89. Hubmaier, "Ban," 418; Hubmaier, "Schriften," 373.
90. Hubmaier, "Ban," 419; Hubmaier, "Schriften," 373.
91. Hubmaier, "Ban," 423; Hubmaier, "Schriften," 377.

on this subject will be offered in chapter 4. For now, however, the import of properly understanding and practicing church discipline within the local church in the theology of Balthasar Hubmaier cannot be overstated because it accomplishes two things: it provides an opportunity for the offender to be reminded of the commitment that he made to the local assembly, and it keeps the church pure and uncorrupted from the sinful attitudes of the one going astray.

The ensuing exposition of the importance of church discipline for the theology of Hubmaier will take place in the following order. As Hubmaier's understanding of the makeup of a man is essential to understanding the whole of his theology, chapter 2 will explore the trichotomous anthropology of the Radical Reformer and its connection to church discipline. Hubmaier's doctrine of salvation for example, which will be considered in chapter 3, was developed, as Mabry points out, not out of the "Pauline theology of the Magisterial Reformers, nor from the Anabaptists' interpretation of the [G]ospels," but in relation to his own anthropology.[92]

In considering the Waldshut preacher's soteriology, this doctrine will be placed within the larger context of the soteriological debate of the sixteenth century. A brief survey of the major reformers' ideas on justification and faith will be provided. Under the larger umbrella of soteriology, such concepts of Hubmaier's theology as "justification" and "sanctification" will be closely examined. Church discipline's intersection and import to the reformer's understanding of salvation will be demonstrated in this chapter.

It is the ordinances of the church, in Hubmaier's theology, that play a major role in the exercise of church discipline. Chapter 4 will evaluate the link between Hubmaier's doctrine of church discipline and ecclesiology focusing on the ordinances. What is of particular interest regarding the reformer's understanding of church discipline is not only its connection to the two ordinances, namely, baptism and the Lord's Supper, but especially its association of the ordinances with the keys. A summary of the argument of this book and conclusions will be offered in chapter 5.

This introduction would not be complete without a word regarding the present limitations. Here it bears mention that, although he was a systematic thinker, according to Rempel, "Hubmaier did not stay with most

---

92. Mabry, *Doctrine of the Church*, 107.

of his themes long enough to develop them into full-fledged doctrines."[93] An attempt to collect and systematize the reformer's thoughts in the areas of anthropology; soteriology, including justification and sanctification; and ecclesiology, therefore, will be made with the utmost care and sensitivity to his immediate context. But there will also be an understanding that, due to Hubmaier's description as someone "who stood between the various views [of the Reformation] but belonged to none of them,"[94] even the utmost experts in the field must offer some educated conjectures regarding the Anabaptist leader's doctrinal positions, particularly in those areas to which he did not devote much attention.

With this in mind, it is now time to dive into the sea of Hubmaier's tripartite anthropology in order to discover its intimate correlation with his understanding of church discipline.

---

93. Rempel, *The Supper*, 42.
94. Westin and Bergsten, *Schriften*, 57.

2

Church Discipline and Anthropology

LATE-MEDIEVAL INFLUENCES IN HUBMAIER'S THEOLOGY

PROPER CONSIDERATION OF BALTHASAR Hubmaier's theology must begin with the exploration of his trichotomous anthropology. It is essential to begin with this examination of the reformer's anthropology because his understanding of the makeup of a man is an integral part of understanding the whole of his theology. As such, the Radical Reformer's doctrine of salvation for example, which will be considered in the next chapter, was developed, as Mabry points out, not out of the "Pauline theology of the magisterial reformers, nor from the Anabaptist interpretation of the Gospels," but in relation to his own anthropology.[1] In the process of the current investigation, the doctrine of church discipline will emerge as an important component in the Radical Reformer's doctrine of man and a significant factor contributing to the formation of Hubmaier's anthropology.

Although it was the purpose of the previous chapter to delineate Hubmaier's theological influences, a full appreciation of his anthropology requires a more detailed examination of the medieval concepts that formed the background for the reformer's high view of the human being. To assume that Hubmaier was simply a product or a disciple of the

1. Mabry, *Doctrine of the Church*, 107.

Church Discipline and Anthropology

teachings of any one of his theological acquaintances, or of all of them collectively would be wrong, for the Radical Reformer's theology seems to be an independently developing line of thought, emerging out of many influences, not the least of which were those concepts that formed the basis of the medieval period in which he operated.[2] Among these concepts were the mainstreams of late-medieval philosophical and theological thought: Humanism, scholasticism and nominalism, and late-medieval Augustinianism, to all of which Hubmaier was exposed as early as during his Freiburg years.[3] In other words, any consideration of the theology of Balthasar Hubmaier apart from his Catholic roots is incomplete at best and misleading at worst. For one should not forget that, in the words of James McClendon, Jr., "John Eck was his Catholic teacher and *Doktorvater*, Regensburg and Waldshut were his Catholic parishes; the Catholic mass was his spiritual wet nurse; Catholic social theory was the leitmotif of his politics of liberty."[4] Considering the vastness of the subjects of late-medieval philosophy and theology, only those concepts which pertain to the general focus of this research will be examined more closely in the following pages.

As to the popular religious climate preceding Hubmaier's day, the research conducted by Alister McGrath for his 1987 volume entitled *The Intellectual Origins of the European Reformation* revealed that in the century predating the Reformation there was an increase in interest in the Christian religion in western Europe.[5] While there was a growing anticlericalism in many European cities, the development of this phenomenon was due partly to the rise in piety and theological awareness on the part of the laity, which led, in turn, to a growing dissatisfaction with the role allocated to the clergy in the order of salvation.[6] The new movement of more pious religion and learning founded by Gerard Groote (1340–84) of Deventer[7] and later known as *devotio moderna*, beginning with the

---

2. Ibid., 3.
3. Ibid., 6.
4. McClendon, "Balthasar Hubmaier," 72.
5. McGrath, *The Intellectual Origins of the European Reformation*, 9.
6. Ibid., 10.
7. Groote believed in a combination of religion and learning. He wanted people to be able to read the Bible, and began to translate parts of it into the vernacular. He sought and advocated a more personal religious experience based on the imitation of Christ. He was a mystic to whom the visible church mattered less than a close union with God. Love,

major monasteries of the Brethren of the Common Life and eventually becoming intermingled with such institutions as the universities of Paris and Tübingen, rapidly assumed a major pedagogical role in the fifteenth century.[8] The precepts of *devotio moderna*, the most famous literary product of which was a manuscript attributed to Thomas à Kempis entitled *The Imitation of Christ*,[9] not only foreshadowed Martin Luther's concept of justification by faith, but also profoundly affected Erasmus, in whom many of its ideas were represented and through whom they reached a wide public.[10] While Erasmus' influence on Hubmaier may be presently debated, as was revealed in chapter 1, the same chapter also exposed a considerable amount of interaction between the two theologians, which enabled a free flow of ideas between them, allowing the assumption that Hubmaier too may have grasped the notions of *The Imitation of Christ* from Erasmus.

The era preceding the sixteenth-century Reformation also witnessed a rising hostility towards scholasticism in theology. The success of Erasmus' *Enchiridion Militis Christiani*, published in the first decades of the sixteenth century, was due in large part to his giving voice to an anti-scholastic notion through his criticisms of scholastic theology.[11] Of course, factors like the advent of printing and the increase in the number of intelligent and literate laity most likely added to its success as well.

Within the Catholic Church the crisis of authority loomed heavily in the late fourteenth to early fifteenth centuries. The Great Schism of 1378–1417, following the death of Gregory XI, the last Avignonese pope, culminated in the recognition of three rival claimants to the papacy in the aftermath of the Council of Pisa in 1409.[12] This schism within the church brought with it a great deal of confusion and anxiety and became a major contributing factor towards further destabilization of control, preparing

---

faith, and humility were all important, far above outward works. It was the devil who told men that good works would bring salvation and persuaded them to do such works, Gilbert, *Renaissance and Reformation*, chapter 9.

8. McGrath, *The Intellectual Origins of the European Reformation*, 10.

9. Though its authorship has been much disputed, it seems to embody material coming out of the circle of the first Brethren of the Common Life, and it undoubtedly represents the ideas and ideals of the movement, Gilbert, *Renaissance and Reformation*.

10. Gilbert, *Renaissance and Reformation*.

11. Erasmus, *Novvm Testamentvm*, 926D–927B.

12. McGrath, *The Intellectual Origins of the European Reformation*, 14.

the soil for the reforming movements of the sixteenth century. McGrath aptly describes the dilemma facing every rank of the Catholic hierarchy at this point in history:

> To whom should believers look for an authoritative, or even a provisional, statement concerning the faith of the church? In a period of unprecedented expansion in theological speculation in the universities and religious houses of Western Europe, guidance was urgently required as to the catholicity of the new methods and doctrines that were emerging. The traditional method of validation of such opinions was by reference to the teaching of the institutional church, objectified in the episcopacy and papacy—yet the institution of the church itself appeared to many to be called into question by the events of the Great Schism, and the period immediately preceding it . . . The development of the astonishing doctrinal diversity of the late fourteenth and fifteenth centuries is probably largely due to the apparent suspension of the normal methods of validation of theological opinions, together with an apparent reluctance (or inability) on the part of the ecclesiastical authorities to take decisive action against heterodox views as and when they arose. The weakening in the fifteenth century of the means by which orthodoxy might be enforced became more pronounced in the first half of the sixteenth century, as factors . . . leading to the erosion of such centralized power as had previously existed at this crucial period in history . . . [resulted] in that the new reforming movements were allowed to develop with minimal hindrance.[13]

The resolution of this matter was believed to be possible only through the convening of an ecumenical council, which was assembled in 1414 and lasted some three years. The Council of Constance is credited with ending the Great Schism by electing Martin V as the new pope on November 11, 1417. Its method, however, further complicated the answer to the question to which office belonged the final authority within the church.[14] Was it to rest with the pope, a council or perhaps even a

---

13. Ibid., 14–15.

14. The fifth session of the Council enacted the decree *Haec sancta*, which affirmed that its authority was derived directly from Christ, and was to be respected even by popes. The ensuing papal opposition to this decree culminated in Pius II's 1460 bull *Execrabilis* in which he reinstated papal authority on the basis of John 21:16, proclaiming the pope to be the only vicar of Jesus Christ and thereby condemning all appeals to councils and prohibiting them as erroneous and detestable.

professor of theology? "It was this uncertainty," according to McGrath, "which contributed, to no small extent, to the remarkable doctrinal diversity of the late medieval church."[15]

Humanism

With regard to the Humanism to which Hubmaier was exposed in Freiburg and later in his interaction with such adherents of the movement as Wolfgang Rychard, John Sapidus, Johann Adelphi, and Erasmus, it was heavily indebted to the Humanism of Italy, yet distinguished by a greater emphasis on social reform.[16] "The reform program of northern Humanism was a broad one," according to the former Kansas University historian Bill Gilbert, "it aimed at a regeneration of moral and spiritual life, of political and ecclesiastical institutions, and of education."[17] The reform of education was the number one emphasis of the northern Humanism, reinstating the classics of Greece, Rome and early Christianity in the process and thereby encouraging the rise in interest in learning Greek and Hebrew languages.

Hubmaier's initial exposure to Humanism was through Eck at Freiburg. Later in Regensburg, Hubmaier met Wolfgang Rychard, who was not only one of the leading Humanists of the day, but was also a leader of the evangelical reformation in Ulm. Torsten Bergsten even suggests that Rychard was responsible for introducing Hubmaier to the writings of Luther and Oecolampadius.[18] In a letter to Sapidus, written in October of 1521, Hubmaier expressed a desire to become better acquainted with the Humanist and asked for his help in getting to know others of a like-minded persuasion. In July of 1522, Hubmaier wrote to another leading Humanist, Johann Adelphi, who was a lay preacher and the counterpart of Rychard in Ulm. In this letter Hubmaier inquired whether the lectures of Melanchton and Luther would serve as good commentaries for Paul's letters to Rom. and to the Cor., which he had been reading.[19]

---

15. McGrath, *The Intellectual Origins of the European Reformation*, 6.

16. Trinkaus, "The Religious Thought of the Italian Humanists, and the Reformers: Anticipation or Autonomy?"

17. Gilbert, *Renaissance and Reformation*.

18. Bergsten, *Hubmaier*, 19.

19. Ibid., 18.

Scholasticism

That Hubmaier was exposed to scholasticism, both at Freiburg and Ingolstadt, can be known not only from historical data of the contemporaneous university curricula, but also from his own writings in which he mentioned specific theologians belonging to the scholastic movement. Among them were such men as Duns Scotus, Thomas Aquinas, William Occam, Gabriel Biel, Robert Holkot, and John Major of Haddington.[20]

Scholasticism is often either quickly dismissed or glossed over in the discussion of the sixteenth-century Reformation because of how it was regarded by most people in that era: as pointless, arid, intellectual speculation over trivia. The term "Scholasticism" itself was used by Humanists to refer disparagingly to the ideas of the "uninteresting period of stagnation between the cultural magnificence of antiquity and its revival during the Renaissance," also known as the Middle Ages.[21] Although difficult to define precisely, scholasticism, according to Alister E. McGrath, "is best regarded as the medieval movement, flourishing in the period 1200–1500, which placed emphasis upon the rational justification of religious beliefs and the systematic presentation of those beliefs."[22] Scholasticism, therefore, does not refer to a specific system of beliefs, but to a particular way of organizing theology.[23] The University of Paris, quickly becoming the intellectual center of Europe, was perhaps one of the most important centers of dissemination of scholasticism on that continent.

The origin of the scholastic movement at the close of the Dark Ages resulted from the rediscovery of Aristotle and his ideas in order to systematize and expand Christian theology and to demonstrate its inherent rationality. Reinhold Seeburg identifies succinctly the key players within the scholastic movement: "The Lombard brought the materials together; Thomas framed definitions; Duns built up and demolished arguments; Occam advocated the positively valid, though not without robbing it of the nimbus of rationality," with Gabriel Biel being "the last important representative of this tendency."[24] Thomas Aquinas and Duns Scotus

---

20. Hubmaier, "Eighteen Theses," 33; Hubmaier, "Schriften," 73; Hubmaier, "A Simple Instruction," 320; Hubmaier, "Schriften," 291; Hubmaier, "Catechism," 343; Hubmaier, "Schriften," 309.

21. McGrath, *Reformation Thought*, 19.

22. Ibid.

23. Ibid.

24. Seeberg, *The History of Doctrines*, 185–86.

helped to establish Aristotelianism as, in their view, the best method for grounding and developing Christian theology and demonstrating the rationality of Christian faith.[25] There is in the writings of these and other representatives of Scholasticism "a sort of serenity born of the confidence" felt by them that, "if properly understood, philosophy was on the side of theology and reason in fundamental harmony with revelation."[26]

The essence of scholasticism, therefore, as summarized by McGrath, was in the "demonstration of the inherent rationality of Christian theology by an appeal to philosophy and the demonstration of the complete harmony of that theology by the minute examination of the relationship of its various elements."[27] That which is "unchurchly" was condemned within scholasticism as being unreasonable, and that which is "churchly" was proved to be reasonable by the intricate methods of dialectics.[28]

To comprehend more fully the complexities of medieval scholasticism requires a basic understanding of the difference between "realism," which dominated the early part of the scholastic period (c.1200–c.1350), and "nominalism," which dominated its later part (c.1350–c.1500).[29] Realism affirmed the existence of invisible universals, concepts that exist on a different metaphysical plane and to which all the particular visible objects conform. Thomism and Scotism, derived from the writings of Thomas Aquinas and Duns Scotus respectively, were the two major scholastic schools influenced by realism in the early medieval period. Nominalism, by contrast, denied the necessity of universals and focused on the particulars as present in the mind alone without the necessity of their independent existence outside the mind.[30] Nominalists had no intention of abandoning Aristotle but focused on following a new way of interpreting his philosophy.[31]

---

25. McGrath, *Reformation Thought*, 69. For example, Aquinas' proof for God's existence using his argument from motion relies completely on an Aristotelian axiom, that everything which moves is moved by something else.

26. Gilson, *History of Christian Philosophy*, 325.

27. McGrath, *Reformation Thought*, 69.

28. Seeberg, *The History of Doctrines*, 105.

29. McGrath, *Reformation Thought*, 71.

30. Ibid., 71–72. For a more detailed discussion of nominalism in late medieval theology, see McGrath, *The Intellectual Origins of the European Reformation*, 70–75.

31. Gilson, *History of Christian Philosophy*, 499.

One of the more popular nominalist motifs, of which Hubmaier avails himself, is the dialectic of the two powers of God, namely His *potentia absoluta*, or "absolute power" and *potentia ordinata*, or "ordained power." According to absolute power, God, "inasmuch as he is omnipotent, has the ability to do many things that he does not will to do, has never done, nor ever will do."[32] *Potentia ordinata*, on the other hand, is the total ordained will of God, the complete plan of God for his creation.[33] One of the main functions of this distinction, particularly as it was found in the theology of Thomas Aquinas, was to affirm that God did not act of necessity; he could have done things other than those he chose to do.[34]

Within nominalism there were three distinct schools of thought, which, aside from their rejection of the necessity of universals, agreed on virtually nothing else.[35] For the purposes of the present work, however, only two of the three will be given careful consideration. One of these schools, now known as the *via moderna*,[36] was highly optimistic concerning human abilities; the other, *schola Augustiniana moderna*,[37] was considerably more pessimistic regarding the matter.[38] This work will now consider the two schools and their influence on Hubmaier in greater detail.

32. Courtenay, "Nominalism and Late Medieval Religion," 37.

33. Ibid., 39.

34. Ibid., 38.

35. There were actually three distinct schools within late scholasticism: first, conservative Augustinian branch of late medieval thought, or right-wing nominalism including such figures as Thomas Bradwardine, Gregory of Rimini, and Hugolino Malbranche of Orvieto; second, the moderate, central, or middle branch of late medieval thought, also called moderate nominalism, including Ockham, Pierre d'Ailly, and Gabriel Biel; and third, the radical branch of late medieval thought, or left-wing nominalism, also known as modernism, including Robert Holcot, Adam Wodham, Nicholas of Autrecourt, Courtenay, "Nominalism and Late Medieval Religion," 34–35. It is the first and third of these, however, that particularly pertain to the focus of the present research. For more on nominalism, see Courtenay, "Nominalism and Late Medieval Religion," 39–51.

36. "The modern way." It is customary to divide the doctrines taught during the second part of the fourteenth century into two classes, according to whether their authors were following the "old way" (*via antiqua*) or the "modern way." The initiator of the modern way is commonly considered to be William of Ockham and the essential feature of his new way is called "nominalism." In other words, the nominalism of the new way is considered as having opposed everywhere the realism of the old way in the main universities and schools of Europe, Gilson, *History of Christian Philosophy*, 487.

37. "The modern Augustinian school."

38. McGrath, *Reformation Thought*, 73.

As it began to make significant inroads into many northern European universities during the fifteenth century, the *via moderna* was a part of Hubmaier's education at Freiburg. At the University of Freiburg the future Radical was exposed to *via moderna's* main adherents in the fourteenth and fifteenth centuries, among whom were William of Ockham, Pierre d'Ailly, Robert Holcot, and Gabriel Biel. In addition to its philosophical nominalism, the movement adopted a doctrine of justification which was branded as Pelagian by many of its critics.[39] The central element of the soteriology of the *via moderna* is a covenant between God and humanity, styled after the contemporaneous idea of a political covenant between a king and his people.[40] This covenant, unilaterally imposed by God, established the conditions necessary for justification.[41] According to the covenant, a man will only be accepted by God if he first fulfills certain demands. God was obligated by the self-imposed terms of the covenant[42] to accept those people who met these demands, known in Latin as *facere quod in se est*.[43] The theologians of the *via moderna* countered the claim to have simply copied Pelagian theology, which resulted from the obvious parallels between their theology and that of Pelagius[44] by drawing upon contemporary economic theory.[45] McGrath quotes William J. Courtenay's account of the classic example of the king and the small lead coin that was invariably cited by the theologians of the *via moderna* to illustrate the relation between good works and justification:

> Most medieval coinage systems used gold and silver coins. This had the advantage of guaranteeing the value of the coins . . .

---

39. Ibid., 76.

40. For more discussion of the nominalist idea of the covenant between God and men, see Steinmetz, "Nominalist Motifs in Hubmaier," 126–27.

41. McGrath, *Reformation Thought*, 76.

42. *facienti quod in se est Deus non denegat gratiam*—"God will not deny his grace to anyone who does what lies within them."

43. "Doing what lies within you," or "doing your best," this concept was also called *synderesis*. According to Gabriel Biel, through a close interrelation of natural and written law, man should be able to achieve by "doing what is in him" a virtuous life. His free will is presented with advice derived from innate, indestructible moral principles, Biel, *Epitome*, S.II.39.C.

44. Both the theologians of the *via moderna* and Pelagius asserted that men and women were accepted on the basis of their own efforts and achievements. Further, both asserted that human works placed God under an obligation to reward them.

45. McGrath, *Reformation Thought*, 76–77.

Occasionally, however, kings found themselves in a financial crisis, through war for example. A standard way of meeting this was to recall gold and silver coins and melt them down. The gold and silver thus retrieved could be used to finance a war.

In the meantime, however, currency of some sort was still required. To meet this need, small leaden coins were issued, which bore the same face value as the gold and silver coins. Although their *inherent* value was negligible, their *ascribed* or *imposed* value was considerable. The king would promise to replace the lead coins with their gold or silver equivalents once the financial crisis was past. The value of the lead coins thus resided in the king's promise to redeem them at their full ascribed value at a later date. The value of a gold coin derives from the gold; but the value of a lead coin derives from the royal covenant to treat that coin *as if it were gold*.[46]

Human works, according to the theologians of the *via moderna*, were, like lead coins, of little inherent value. What gave them value, however, was God's promise, through the covenant, to treat them as if they were of much greater value, in just the same way as a king could treat a lead coin as if it were gold. Pelagius, on the other hand, treated human works as if they were gold, capable of purchasing salvation. Thus, "the theological exploitation of the difference between the inherent and the imposed value of coins," according to McGrath, "served to get the theologians of the *via moderna* out of a potentially awkward situation."[47]

Late-Medieval Augustinianism

The University of Oxford was both one of the strongholds of the *via moderna* and the place from which the first backlash against it occurred. Thomas Bradwardine, who was later to become Archbishop of Canterbury, was the man responsible for the backlash.[48] Bradwardine's ideas were taken up on the mainland of Europe by Gregory of Rimini at the University of Paris, who happened to be a member of the Order of the Hermits of St. Augustine, elsewhere referred to as the Augustinian Order.[49] It was Gregory of Rimini's ideas, then, promoted by the Augustinians,

46. Ibid., 76–77.

47. McGrath, *Reformation Thought*, 77–78. For more discussion of *via moderna*, see McGrath, *The Intellectual Origins of the European Reformation*, 75–85.

48. For more on Bradwardine, see Seeberg, *The History of Doctrines*, 7–8.

49. McGrath, *Reformation Thought*, 78.

that became known as the *schola Augustiniana moderna*, "the modern Augustinian school," and to which Hubmaier was partially reacting in his understanding of the doctrines of man and salvation.[50] What were the general precepts of this tradition?

First, Gregory adopted a nominalist view on the question of universals.[51] Having no time for the realism of Thomas Aquinas or Duns Scotus, in this respect Gregory actually had much in common with thinkers of the *via moderna*, such as Robert Holcot and Gabriel Biel. Second, Gregory's soteriology reflected an Augustinian influence in its emphasis on the need for grace, on the fallenness and sinfulness of humanity, on the divine initiative in justification, and on divine predestination.[52] Below are some of the major points of the theology of Augustine of Hippo to which Gregory was indebted:

(a) God created man good and upright.

(b) All of this Adam lost in the fall becoming a sinner.

(c) This character of Adam has now passed over to his posterity.

(d) The corruption of the body which oppresses the soul is the penalty of the first sin.

(e) The salvation of men is attributed to grace alone.

(f) The chief work of grace is really the infusion of love or of a new and good will by the Holy Spirit.

(g) Grace, as being irresistible, is characterized as predestinating grace.[53]

Salvation, in Gregory's understanding, was totally a work of God, from its beginning to its end. In fact, all the necessary soteriological resources were located exclusively outside human nature, according to Gregory of Rimini, including the ability to desist from sin and turn to righteousness, which too arose through the action of God.[54]

50. For more on Gregory of Rimini, see Gilson, *History of Christian Philosophy*, 502–3.

51. McGrath, *Reformation Thought*, 78.

52. Ibid., 79. See also Marrou, *St. Augustine and His Influence through the Ages*; Seeberg, *The History of Doctrines*, 307–67.

53. Seeberg, *The History of Doctrines*, 341–50; Augustin, "On the Merits and Remission of Sins, and on the Baptism of Infants," I.2, 8–9, 13, 19; Augustine, "On the Grace of Christ, and on Original Sin," I.13, 15, 22, 27; Augustine, "On the Predestination of the Saints," I.19.

54. McGrath, *Reformation Thought*, 9. For a more detailed discussion of the

Such was the time and the theological background which contributed to shaping the theology of Balthasar Hubmaier. It bears mention here, again, that as a thinker and a theologian in his own right, Hubmaier did not blindly embrace everything to which he was exposed, but, moved by his desire to ground everything in the Word of God, selected only those ideas which he felt were in agreement with Scripture. A comparison of Hubmaier's theology with that of his Catholic teacher Eck serves as a good example of this claim. Walter Moore identifies extensive common ground between Eck and Hubmaier. Yet he notes that one of Hubmaier's most distinctive features, namely his tripartite anthropology cannot be found anywhere in Eck's writings.[55] John Rempel's commentary on this phenomenon is befitting: "Moore's point . . . should be accepted as a caution against trying to identify Hubmaier completely with any one theology or trying to locate all his notions in the writings of known theologians."[56]

HUBMAIER'S ANTHROPOLOGY

Reflecting his medieval theological background, Hubmaier has a high view of the human being. Hubmaier's anthropology, therefore, aside from its biblical support, draws more from the medieval motifs then the Augustinian understanding of his Magisterial counterparts. As such, his beliefs about human nature stand in especially sharp contrast to those of Luther and Calvin. Henry C. Vedder communicates this idea quite precisely when he states that "what Hübmaier sought was escape from the paralysing Augustinianism of Luther; and he [Hubmaier] attempted to work out a theory that should make a reality and not an empty form of the preaching of the gospel."[57] Luther's anthropology, seeking to magnify the divine grace, cast unregenerate man as completely blind and unable even to respond in faith to the free gift of salvation:

> But a man cannot be thoroughly humbled, until he comes to know that his salvation is utterly beyond his own powers, counsel, endeavors, will, and works, and absolutely depending on the will,

---

Augustinian theology and influences in the late medieval era, see McGrath, *The Intellectual Origins of the European Reformation*, 86–93.

55. Moore, "Eck & Hubmaier," 80.
56. Rempel, *The Supper*, 43.
57. Vedder, *Hübmaier*, 193.

counsel, pleasure, and work of another, that is, of God only. For if, as long as he has any persuasion that he can do even the least thing himself towards his own salvation, he retain a confidence in himself and do not utterly despair in himself, so long he is not humbled before God; but he proposes to himself some place, some time, or some work, whereby he may at length attain unto salvation. But he who hesitates not to depend wholly upon the goodwill of God, he totally despairs in himself, chooses nothing for himself, but waits for God to work in him; and such an one, is the nearest unto grace, that he might be saved.[58]

Alvin J. Beachy clarifies the picture of Luther's position when he claims that "the Magisterial Reformers arrived at their concept of grace through an anthropology that centered in the bondage of the will and the doctrine of predestination."[59] The doctrine taught by Luther and his followers then, as recapitulated by Vedder, was that "in spiritual things the unregenerate man is wholly blind, unable to work the righteousness of God, and his will has become utterly hostile to God, so that he cannot by his own powers give any assistance or co-operation towards his own salvation."[60] Vedder provides a powerful illustration of Luther's understanding of man's utter inability to contribute in any way to the process of his salvation: "He is a man in the rapids of Niagara, being swept towards destruction, not only unable to do anything to help himself, but unable even to grasp the rope thrown to him by a friendly hand,—nay, not even desiring to be saved, and must against his will be dragged ashore, kicking and struggling against his rescuer to the last."[61] For Luther, allowing man the ability to participate was tantamount to the idea of salvation by works. Hubmaier, however, could not understand the need for all the invitations of the gospel if man cannot possibly heed them. Robert Friedmann summarizes this aspect of Hubmaier's freedom of the will in the following words, "If God commands His way, man must be able to obey such commandments after experiencing rebirth and the restoration of man's freedom in God's image."[62]

---

58. Martin Luther, *The Bondage of the Will*, 7.24.
59. Beachy, *Grace in the Radical Reformation*, 33.
60. Vedder, *Hübmaier*, 196.
61. Ibid.
62. Friedmann, *The Theology of Anabaptism: An Interpretation*, 60.

Church Discipline and Anthropology

In contrast to the heavy reliance on Augustinian categories within the anthropologies of the Magisterial Reformers, Hubmaier reaches back to a number of late-medieval scholastic concepts with which to support his doctrine of man. His major support is derived from Scripture, so at least the Anabaptist leader is consistent in his desire to ground all doctrine in the Word of God. In places where Hubmaier sees contradiction between the different ideas pertaining to anthropology taught in the Bible, he relies on the following nominalistic concepts. First, Hubmaier rejects the doctrine of predestination. "From the vantage point of his older anthropology," according to Rempel, "Hubmaier was convinced that belief in both the bondage of the will and predestination violates the biblical picture of the human will and undermines human responsibility before God."[63] With regard to Luther's Augustinianism, therefore, Hubmaier wishes to affirm the Augustinian understanding of prevenient grace, while at the same time rejecting the Augustinian understanding of predestination.[64] Second, Hubmaier promotes the dialectic of the two powers of God, the idea that originated in the thirteenth century and was popularized in the writings of Thomas Aquinas. In his *On Freedom of the Will, II*, Hubmaier's discussion of God's free choice of Isaac and rejection of Esau causes him to utilize the concepts of the revealed and secret will of God, which are not only reminiscent of the Thomistic *potentia absoluta* and *potentia ordinata*, but also seem to depend to a certain extent on Gabriel Biel's discussion of the will of God and human will.[65] To use the words of David Steinmetz, "both in his doctrine of the dialectic of the two powers of God and in his view of predestination," Hubmaier "has revived the nominalistic solutions and embraced them as his own."[66] Fourth, the direction of his unfallen will is reminiscent of the synderesis, since it is "the inclination toward first principles and not the application of the practical reason which Hubmaier has principally in mind."[67] Fifth, Hubmaier makes use of the *via moderna's* principle, *facere quod in se est*, which, according to David Steinmetz, operates for the Anabaptist leader

---

63. Rempel, *The Supper*, 45.

64. Hubmaier particularly rejects the aspect of the doctrine which nullifies any human responsibility in the salvific transaction.

65. Biel, *Epitome*, II.37.I.F; Hubmaier, "Freedom of the Will, II," 471–82; Hubmaier, "Schriften," 416–25.

66. Steinmetz, "Nominalist Motifs in Hubmaier," 131.

67. Ibid., 133.

on two levels: "(a) the level of reason and revelation, and (b) the level of grace and free will. Man does not need to wait for the proclamation of the gospel and illumination by the Holy Spirit before some response is possible. The heathen, who have never heard the gospel, have two resources for the return to God: (1) the unfallen will of the spirit . . . and (2) the revelation of God in nature."[68]

Those who respond to the general revelation of God in nature and who long to know Him will be granted the opportunity to be saved through the external proclamation of the Word, whether through ordinary messengers or even angels, if need be.[69] It must be pointed out, however, that not every sinner returns to God on the basis of *facere quod in se est*. With some, God takes initiative and gives them the invitation to salvation by grace alone. Hubmaier's rejection of Augustinian predeterminism keeps the sinner from being utterly dependent on the initiative of God for gaining that knowledge of the gospel which will make salvation possible.[70] Sixth, Hubmaier reaches back to the doctrine of the covenant, making it the link between the unlimited freedom of God and the limited freedom of man.[71] Steinmetz aptly describes Hubmaier's dependence on this medieval concept:

> By making use of his limited freedom, the sinner disposes his will for the reception of grace, which cannot be given to him without his free and uncoerced consent. When the sinner responds to the offer of the gospel, God *must* generate him, not because of the quality of his response but because God has bound himself by his promise to justify those who respond to the gospel. God is a captive of his own covenant; the freedom of his absolute power has been imprisoned by his ordained will.[72]

Thus the God of both Biel and Hubmaier is "a God who manifests toward the sinner fidelity to his covenant."[73] While Steinmetz accurately assesses Hubmaier's reliance on certain medieval concepts for his

---

68. Steinmetz, "Nominalist Motifs in Hubmaier," 134; Hubmaier, "Freedom, I," 437; Hubmaier, "Schriften," 388.

69. Hubmaier, "Freedom, I," 437–38; Hubmaier, "Schriften," 388–89.

70. Steinmetz, "Nominalist Motifs in Hubmaier," 135.

71. Ibid.

72. Steinmetz, "Nominalist Motifs in Hubmaier," 135–36; Hubmaier, "Freedom of the Will, II," 473–75; Hubmaier, "Schriften," 417–18.

73. Steinmetz, "Nominalist Motifs in Hubmaier," 136.

anthropology, his final evaluation of the Radical's theological position as semi-Pelagian must be rejected. In borrowing A. H. Newman's terminology, this author would prefer to call Hubmaier semi-Augustinian instead.[74] That which Steinmetz identifies as semi-Pelagianism should be regarded as the tension in Hubmaier's theology between God's grace and man's responsibility, which is the overall tenor of the Anabaptist leader's thought in accordance with his understanding of the overall message of Scripture.[75] Should Hubmaier have had more time and freedom to develop his thinking on the subject, he would have clarified and sharpened his doctrine of man, particularly as pertains to this area.

Hubmaier's anthropology therefore centers in the freedom of the will, via scholastic categories and heavy reliance upon the Pauline distinction between flesh, soul, and spirit. His trichotomous anthropology allows him to hold that humans are not completely corrupted by the fall and original sin.[76] As a trichotomist, the Radical Reformer views men as consisting of three parts: spirit, soul, and body. This, Hubmaier earnestly believed, was the plain teaching of the Scripture. From the very first lines of his *Freedom of the Will, I*, Hubmaier introduces biblical support for his tripartite anthropology. He looks to Gen 2:7 for three distinct elements which together make up three parts of man, namely the flesh, being made out of earth or dust; the living breath, the Hebrew term also translated as "spirit"; and the soul: "When the Lord God made the human being out of the dust from the earth, he blew a living breath into his face and thus the human being became a living soul, Gen 2:7. Here Moses points to three things with distinct names. First, the flesh or the body is made out of the earth,... Second,... the living breath,... Third, the soul,... is expressed separately; it is that which makes the body alive."[77]

Perhaps the key New Testament text upon which he based his particular anthropological understanding was 1 Thess 5:23. To these two texts, the Radical Reformer adds the distinction between the soul and the spirit in Heb 4:12; Mary's distinction between soul, spirit, and misery, which Hubmaier understands to refer to flesh, in Luke 1:46; and Jesus'

---

74. Newman, *Church History*, II–468. Incidentally Thomas N. Finger agrees with this description of Hubmaier's anthropology in his *A Contemporary Anabaptist Theology*, Finger, *A Contemporary Anabaptist Theology*, 469–70.

75. For more on this, see Rempel's helpful discussion in Rempel, *The Supper*, 83.

76. Mabry, *Doctrine of the Church*, 110.

77. Hubmaier, "Freedom, I," 429–30; Hubmaier, "Schriften," 382.

separation of the three elements in his statement to the disciples on the Mount of Olives in Matt 26:41. In the last passage Hubmaier believes that when Jesus was praying in the Garden of Gethsemane, the will of the flesh caused Him to ask the Father to remove the cup of suffering from Him, but the Spirit enabled Jesus to end with, "not my will, but yours be done." Hubmaier's trinitarian view of the Matt 26:41 passage, therefore, induces him to see the trichotomous nature of man as patterned after the Trinity: "Here, Christian reader, you see bright and clear that these three special and essential substances—soul, spirit, and body—are made and unified in every human being according to the image of the Holy Trinity."[78] Resting on his exegesis of Matt 26:41, particularly with respect to Jesus' utterances being in accordance with the will of the flesh and the will of the Spirit, and aided by his understanding of John 1:13, Hubmaier also asserts that each part of the trichotomous nature of man, namely, *Seel, Geist,* and *Leib* (i.e., soul, spirit, and body), has a will of its own: "the will of the flesh, which does not want to suffer; the will of the soul, willing to suffer, but due to the flesh seeks not to; and the will of the spirit which strongly desires to suffer."[79]

Hubmaier further divides his doctrine of man into three separate stages: "(1) the human condition before the Fall; (2) the human condition after the Fall; and (3) the human condition after the restoration through Christ."[80] As all three substances of a man were good prior to the fall, according to Gen 1:31, their wills were in perfect harmony and were "wholly free to choose good or evil, life or death, heaven or hell."[81] A human being before the fall, therefore, had a "free will to will and to perform good or evil,"[82] and was able without additional grace from God to remain in this "inborn innocence and righteousness unto eternal life."[83]

Adam's sin changed the balance of the created condition for the entire human race.[84] The fall brought two wounds upon human beings according to Hubmaier. The first is an inner one which is ignorance of good

---

78. Hubmaier, "Freedom, I," 430; Hubmaier, "Schriften," 383.
79. Hubmaier, "Freedom, I," 431; Hubmaier, "Schriften," 383.
80. Hubmaier, "Freedom, I," 432; Hubmaier, "Schriften," 384.
81. Hubmaier, "Freedom, I," 432; Hubmaier, "Schriften," 385.
82. Hubmaier, "Freedom, I," 433; Hubmaier, "Schriften," 385.
83. Hubmaier, "Freedom, I," 443; Hubmaier, "Schriften," 393.
84. Hubmaier, "Freedom, I," 433; Hubmaier, "Schriften," 385.

and evil. The second wound is external, affecting the doing and acting.[85] Viewing Christ as the Good Samaritan in Luke 10:34, who pours wine and oil on the wounds of the wounded humanity, the Waldshut priest believed that the wine which healed the first wound was the law, "in which the human being by a new grace is again taught anew what is truly good and evil before God."[86] The oil which healed the second wound was the gospel. Both wine and oil are necessary for salvation.

Following the fall of Adam, the flesh was wholly ruined, irretrievably losing its goodness and freedom and becoming completely "worthless and hopeless unto death."[87] In the fall the flesh lost all capability to do anything but sin, constantly striving against God and being the enemy of his commandments. Furthermore, in Hubmaier's view, it is the flesh that is the negative force that keeps men from doing what is right in Rom 7 and 8. As such, the flesh and the blood[88] cannot possess the kingdom of God.[89] Hubmaier believes Eve to be an illustration of our flesh and traces the conception and birth of every man as in sin through her fall: "From the first moment already he is up to his ears in sin and from that moment on when he receives life he begins to die and become earth again."[90] While many of his fellow Anabaptist leaders denied the concept of the original sin,[91] Hubmaier cites passages like Job 3:1; Jer 20:14; and Ps 51:7, in which Job, Jer., and King David curse and lament the time of their birth due to the sinful nature of man.[92] He further makes use of such passages as Rom 7:55ff.; Gal 5:13ff.; 1 Cor 11:27; 15:50; and Matt 16:17, as support for his argument that since the fall the flesh is worthless.

---

85. Hubmaier, "Freedom, I," 445; Hubmaier, "Schriften," 395.
86. Hubmaier, "Freedom, I," 446; Hubmaier, "Schriften," 395.
87. Hubmaier, "Freedom, I," 433; Hubmaier, "Schriften," 385.
88. The blood is of the same will as the flesh, in view of Matt 16:17.
89. Hubmaier, "Freedom, I," 433; Hubmaier, "Schriften," 385.
90. Hubmaier, "Freedom, I," 434; Hubmaier, "Schriften," 386.
91. While the term "original sin" does not appear in the New Testament, the basic idea of the doctrine is found in Pauline epistles, especially Rom 5 and 1 Cor 15. It was Augustine who brought the concept to the forefront of Christian anthropology and soteriology. The doctrine of original sin was mostly bypassed in the Anabaptist literature of the sixteenth century. Of those that did mention it, many, like Hans Denck and Peter Riedemann, rejected it outright. For more detailed discussion of the Anabaptist doctrine of the original sin, see Friedman, "Original Sin".
92. Hubmaier, "Freedom, I," 434; Hubmaier, "Schriften," 386.

The spirit alone remained unaffected by the fall. Alvin J. Beachy describes man's spirit in Hubmaier's anthropology as the only part of man that remains "good and upright and whole as it was before the fall," for it did not consent either by the will, counsel, or act to the eating of the forbidden fruit by the flesh.[93] Hubmaier's own writing confirms the accuracy of Beachy's assessment, "The spirit . . . remained upright, whole, and good. For it has neither with counsel nor deed, will nor action, been disobedient in any way in allowing the flesh to eat the forbidden fruit. Indeed, like a prisoner in the body, it had to eat against its will."[94]

A careful examination of man's fallen condition in Hubmaier's theology reveals some correspondence to Gabriel Biel's anthropological elucidations, as Biel writes:

> Man's wounded nature . . . has to be healed so that man's will, which in principle never lost its freedom of choice, can elicit the meritorious acts required for his acceptation by God . . . Though man may be said to be in a miserable position, enslaved by the law of the flesh which requires that there be a healing aspect to the process of justification, his will is nevertheless free . . . Original sin has primarily a psychological, not an ontological impact on the free will of man . . . [it] does not, however, interfere with the freedom of the will as such.[95]

Although undoubtedly influenced by the medieval understanding of the doctrine of man, Hubmaier's main goal was to focus his theology in Scripture. As such, in order to support his understanding of the spirit's wholeness, the Anabaptist leader focuses on the New Testament passage of 1 Thess 5:23. The second part of the verse contains the following: "I pray God your *whole* spirit and soul and body be preserved blameless unto the coming of our Lord Jesus Christ."[96] Hubmaier's argument from this one passage is that the spirit is in a different case from the body and soul since the fall, because the apostle says here "the whole spirit," but does not say "the whole soul," or "the whole body" for "what has once disintegrated and been shattered is no longer whole."[97] The spirit is, therefore, without

---

93. Beachy, *Grace in the Radical Reformation*, 51.
94. Hubmaier, "Freedom, I," 434; Hubmaier, "Schriften," 386.
95. Oberman, *The Harvest of Medieval Theology*, 128–29.
96. This quotation is from King James Version [emphasis mine].
97. Vedder, *Hübmaier*, 191. This is one of the very few examples where Hubmaier's exegesis is, in Henry S. Vedder's words, "puerile." Although it is claimed that Hubmaier

guilt, for it has retained its original righteousness (*erbgerechtigkeit*) in which it was first created.

The import of the spirit's retention of its freedom becomes instrumental to Hubmaier's doctrine of justification, which will be covered in chapter 3. The Radical Reformer argued that because human nature was in possession of a free will, it was possible for people to repent and accept the grace offered them.[98] In the process of redemption, the soul is united with the spirit, and together they make the flesh their prisoner.[99]

The soul became wounded, in that it lost its knowledge of good and evil, and was "sick unto death, so that it can on its own choose nothing good."[100] Through the fall the soul became flesh or, as Hubmaier states, an Eve. One of the main reasons that the soul can do nothing good is because the flesh, which is its outward instrument, is incapable of doing anything good: "Since the instrument is incapable of doing anything, how can anything good be done with it, even if the soul gladly wanted to and made every effort."[101] The good news for the soul, however, is that its fallen condition is reparable through the Word of God: "That, however, this Fall of the soul is also reparable and harmless here on earth, while that of the flesh irreparable and even deadly, is due to the following: Adam, a figure of the soul—as Eve is a figure of the flesh—would have preferred not to eat of the forbidden tree."[102]

When Adam ate of the tree, he, like our souls, lost the taste of the knowledge of good and evil, so that he can "neither know nor judge what is right, good, or evil before God, or what works are pleasing to God; all this even though he would gladly do right according to the spirit."[103] As mentioned above, God restores the taste for righteousness in those who

---

knew both Greek and Hebrew, he apparently made no use of the original language in his exposition of this passage. For even a quick look at the Greek text reveals that *holoklēron* modifies all three subjects, namely spirit, soul, and body (*kai holoklēron hymōn to pneuma kai hē psychē kai to sōma amemptōs en tē parousia tou kuriou hēmōn Iēsou christou tērēthein*). The same is true of the Vulgate, from which he generally quoted, and in which *integer* modifies spirit, soul, and body (*ut integer spiritus vester, et anima, et corpus sine querela in adventu Domini nostri Jesu Christi servetur*).

98. Rempel, *The Supper*, 44.
99. Hubmaier, "Freedom, I," 439–40; Hubmaier, "Schriften," 390.
100. Hubmaier, "Freedom, I," 435; Hubmaier, "Schriften," 386–87.
101. Hubmaier, "Freedom, I," 435; Hubmaier, "Schriften," 386–87.
102. Hubmaier, "Freedom, I," 435; Hubmaier, "Schriften," 387.
103. Hubmaier, "Freedom, I," 436; Hubmaier, "Schriften," 387.

hunger and thirst after it and ask God for it upon their discernment of his eternal power and divinity displayed in nature. Those who respond to general revelation God will not turn away empty and without instruction, "but will fill them with good things and will also send ambassadors and epistles by which they will be led on the right way of truth."[104] Those, however, who have sinned against the Holy Spirit, according to Hubmaier, will never be able to find God, for they can never have their taste for righteousness renewed. This is then the way the substances are in the human being in Hubmaier's anthropological understanding, before and after the transgression of Adam.

After the restoration by Christ, the flesh is still incapable of doing anything good and is completely ruined. The soul, which is free now, has a choice to make, standing as it were between the flesh and the spirit. The soul can "will and do good, as much as depends on it, for it can command the flesh in such a way that it tames and masters it, so that against its own inclination it must go into fire with the spirit and with the soul on account of the name of Christ."[105] The spirit, which alone was unaffected by the fall of Adam, is whole also after the restoration, rejoicing and doing all that it can to influence the soul in order to take the flesh captive to the obedience of Christ. Hubmaier contends, on the basis of such Scripture passages as Matt 19:7 and Rom 8:13, that true health and freedom must be present in humanity after the restoration or otherwise people will not be able to choose Christ.[106]

This freedom of the will after the restoration within humans is not to be confused with Pelagianism. The distinctive characteristic of Hubmaier's freedom of the will, according to Robert Friedmann's assessment, is that it is "only the freedom of the 'reborn man,' the freedom under divine grace," rather than something "purely moral."[107] God's primacy in salvation is therefore retained within his theology, while, at the same time, man's responsibility is upheld.

Hubmaier's tripartite anthropology causes him to understand the law of the Old Testament as playing different roles for different parts of man: to the flesh the law was given "for the recognition of its sins; to the spirit

---

104. Hubmaier, "Freedom, I," 437; Hubmaier, "Schriften," 388.
105. Hubmaier, "Freedom, I," 441; Hubmaier, "Schriften," 391.
106. Hubmaier, "Freedom, I," 440; Hubmaier, "Schriften," 390.
107. Friedmann, *The Theology of Anabaptism*, 60.

as an aid and witness against sin; to the soul for a light whereby it can see and learn the way of righteousness and flee sin and evil."[108] Similarly each part of man reacts differently to the law: the flesh is frightened, the spirit leaps for joy, while the believing soul thanks God for the enlightenment that it provides. The law further functions as wine, as mentioned above, in the reformer's understanding of the parable of the Good Samaritan. In his Catechism, Hubmaier summarizes his doctrine of man in a clear fashion:

> In sum: First God made us good and free in soul, body, and spirit. This goodness and freedom were through Adam's disobedience taken captive in our spirit, wounded in our soul, and completely corrupted in our flesh; therefore we are all conceived and born in sin and are by nature the children of wrath. If we are now again to become free in the spirit and healthy in the soul, and if this Fall is to be made completely harmless in the flesh, then this must take place through a rebirth as Christ said, or we shall not enter into the kingdom of God.[109]

God the Father, who looks at humanity anew due to the merit of his Son Jesus Christ, draws all men, rather than forcing them, through his life-giving Word which he speaks into people's hearts. Through it all people have power and authority to choose Christ, should they desire to do so.[110] Those who come are able to have a true life transformation through his Word, which is powerful, authoritative, and strong in their lives. Those who do not come seal their fate by their rejection of God's free gift.

The true transformation in the lives of those who come is accomplished through God's Word by means of the Holy Spirit. This statement introduces a distinct understanding of the interrelationship between the Word and the Spirit in the process of redemption of mankind in Hubmaier's theology. "We must be born of water and Spirit," he writes in his *Freedom of the Will, I*, "that is, through the Word of God."[111] Hubmaier understands the Word of God to be water to all who thirst for salvation. Without this water, therefore, salvation is not possible. Cristof Windhorst in his work *Täuferisches Taufverständnis* focuses on this concept in Hubmaier's theology, pointing out that "For Hubmaier, the rebirth,

108. Hubmaier, "Freedom, I," 442; Hubmaier, "Schriften," 393.
109. Hubmaier, "Catechism," 361; Hubmaier, "Schriften," 322–23.
110. Hubmaier, "Freedom, I," 444; Hubmaier, "Schriften," 394.
111. Hubmaier, "Freedom, I," 431; Hubmaier, "Schriften," 383.

as the baptism of the Spirit, is closely bound with the preaching of the word."[112] Those people who earnestly seek salvation, therefore, according to Windhorst's evaluation of Hubmaier's anthropology, God will not send away "empty and without instruction through the word, as in the example of Philip and the Ethiopian treasurer."[113] Bringing Hubmaier's Catechism to fore, Windhorst points to the Anabaptist's similar teaching there that "the wounded and darkened soul of man is raised up again by the preaching of the word and the enlightened soul understands the truth, it has been convinced by the spirit and the preached word."[114]

In evaluating Hubmaier's understanding of the Spirit and the Word, Windhorst reveals its convergence with God's order of salvation recorded in Rom 10:13-17, "where preaching is an essential ministry of the apostles because faith comes through preaching."[115] And again, "according to the sequence of word, faith, baptism, it must go in this order: sending of the preachers, preaching and hearing of the preaching, faith, baptism."[116] Windhorst, however, is quick to acknowledge that Hubmaier exercises great caution to distinguish men's preached word from the Word of God.[117] The latter is used to identify the Scripture, while the former is the link used by God to bring his Word into the

---

112. "für Hubmaier die Wiedergeburt—wie die Geisttaufe—eng mit der Predigt des Wortes verknüpft ist," Windhorst, *Täferisches Taufverständnis*, 187.

113. "Menschen, denen es ernst um ihr Heil ist, bleiben nicht ohne Belehrung durch das Wort, wie das Beispiel von Philippus und dem Kämmerer aus Äthiopien zeigt." Windhorst, *Täferisches Taufverständnis*, 187; Hubmaier, "Freedom, I," 437; Hubmaier, "Schriften," 388.

114. "die verwundete und verfinsterte Seele des Menschen wird durch die Verkündigung des Wortes wieder aufgerichtet, und in der Erleuchtung versteht die Seele die Wahrheit, indem sie durch den Geist und das gepredigte Wort überzeugt worden ist." Windhorst, *Täferisches Taufverständnis*, 187; Hubmaier, "Catechism," 360; Hubmaier, "Schriften," 2.

115. "daß die Predigt ein wesentlicher Bestandteil des Apostelamtes ist; denn durch die Predigt kommt es zum Glauben," Windhorst, *Täferisches Taufverständnis*, 187.

116. "Entsprechend der Folge von Wort—Glaube—Taufe muß es so gehen: Sendung des Predigers, Predigen und Hören der Predigt, Glauben, Taufen." Windhorst, *Täferisches Taufverständnis*, 187; Hubmaier, "Christian Baptism," 116; Hubmaier, "Schriften," 135.

117. "Zwar kann Hubmaier vom 'gepredigten Wort Gottes' sprechen, wie sich eben gezeigt hat. Hier jedoch, im Zusammenhang der Auslegung von Röm 10, redet er nur über die Predigt als Predigtwort der Menschen, nicht aber vom Wort Gottes." Windhorst, *Täferisches Taufverständnis*, 187.

Church Discipline and Anthropology 49

lives of men. There is a fundamental difference between the two.[118] Windhorst observes that in Hubmaier:

> God's word has a direct effect on what it says, but man's does not. It is therefore essential that the sick and sinners must hear the word of Christ himself for their healing and justification, and must learn the power of God`s word, which alone can produce the rebirth.
>
> It is noteworthy that Hubmaier discussed primarily the relationship between the power and work of God's preached word, but did not mention the work of the Spirit. This is not to conclude, on the one hand, that Hubmaier thinks of the work of God's Word and preaching without participation from people, and, on the other hand, it does not mean that the work of God's word is even imaginable without the coming of the Spirit. Instead, here in the context of his entire reflection on the relationship of Word and Spirit, the preaching is thought as an instrument, through which God's Word is heard, and the Spirit, as the force which makes it effective.[119]

Just as people cannot be saved without hearing the preached word of God, the preached word alone cannot save without the Spirit's work in the hearts of men. Hubmaier himself delineates that the Word of God is made alive in us through the Spirit of God, "without whose working it is a killing letter."[120] Windhorst's analysis of Hubmaier's thought is quite accurate here, "preaching the word is necessary, however, it remains ineffective, a

---

118. "Dementsprechend stellt er einen grundsätzlichen 'vnnderschaid zwischen eins menschens wort vnnd dem wort gottes' fest." Windhorst, *Täferisches Taufverständnis*, 190; Hubmaier, "Apologia," 553; Hubmaier, "Schriften," 484.

119. "Gottes Wort wirkt unmittelbar, was es besagt, eines Menschen Wort dagegen nicht. Deshalb ist es für ihn wesentlich, daß der kranke Sünder auch das Wort Christi selbst zu seiner Heilung und Rechtfertigung vernehmen muß, und die Kraft des Gotteswortes selbst erfahren muß, die die Wiedergeburt wirkt.
Bemerkenswert ist, daß Hubmaier in dem hier vornehmlich besprochenen Zusammenhang von der Kraft und Wirkung des göttlichen Wortes die Predigt, aber auch das Wirken des Geistes unerwähnt läßt. Daraus ist jedoch einerseits nich zu schließen, daß Hubmaier die Wirkung des göllichen Wortes ohne Zuspruch und Predigt von Menschen denkt, und andererseits bedeutet das nicht, daß das Wirken des göttlichen Wortes ohne hinzukommenden Geist vorstellbar ist. Vielmehr wird auch hier im Kontext seines gesamten Nachdenkens über das Verhältnis von Wort und Geist die Predigt als Instrument gedacht, das das Gotteswort hörbar, und der Geist als die Kraft, die es wirksam macht." Windhorst, *Täferisches Taufverständnis*, 190.

120. Hubmaier, "Freedom, I," 431; Hubmaier, "Schriften," 384.

killing letter, when God does not direct the work of salvation to follow it, or if this word is not spoken by the Spirit into a living force."[121]

The Radical proceeds to make use of the following passages in supporting his present understanding: Jer 20:14; John 3:5; 4:14; 7:48; 2 Cor 3:6; Rom 8:13; Ps 51:12; Deut 8:3; and Matt 4:4. After salvation, the Holy Spirit also helps and enables the spirit within man to fight victoriously in the battle against flesh, sin, the world, death, the devil, and hell. The Word of God, therefore, quickened by the Holy Spirit, whether leading up to salvation or following it, is always one of the most essential resources, one of the most powerful allies, or the most potent weapon in the arsenal of the spirit of man providing critical assistance in its struggle with the flesh:

> To this end every word that proceeds out of the mouth of God helps the spirit so that the flesh with its evil will and lusts can nowhere flee, hide, or cover itself. It finds outwardly neither rest nor respite before the preached Word of God whose sound goes throughout the whole world, nor internally in the spirit for it is everywhere convicted. Since all testimony is proved in the mouth of two or three witnesses, thence comes the conscience and the gnawing worm into the heart of the human being.[122]

Does Hubmaier's anthropology then seem to be self-contradictory? Does he want, for the sake of his doctrine of the freedom of the will, to have a partially depraved man, and, at the same time, assert that we are poor and miserable sinners?[123] The most probable answer to this question lies within his unique understanding of faith.

Faith, according to Hubmaier's exegesis of John 6:29 in his *On Christian Baptism*, is the work of God.[124] Yet, at the same time, in his *Freedom of the Will, I*, Hubmaier writes thus: "God has created you without your help, but without your help he will not save you."[125] For this multi-faceted concept of faith, Hubmaier must be relying on his Medieval

---

121. "Das Wort als Predigt ist notwendig, bleibt jedoch unwirksam, ein tötender Buchstabe, wenn Gott selbst nicht sein darauf folgendes Heilswerk ausrichtet Order wenn dies gesprochene Wort nicht durch den Geist zu einer lebendigen Kraft wird," Windhorst, *Täferisches Taufverständnis*, 188–89.

122. Hubmaier, "Freedom, I," 431; Hubmaier, "Schriften," 384.

123. Hubmaier, "Christian Baptism," 98; Hubmaier, "Schriften," 120.

124. Hubmaier, "Christian Baptism," 106; Hubmaier, "Schriften," 127.

125. Hubmaier, "Freedom, I," 440; Hubmaier, "Schriften," 391. A more detailed discussion of Hubmaier's faith will be provided in the next chapter.

Church Discipline and Anthropology   51

predecessors, particularly Gabriel Biel's understanding of faith. Biel held to a double aspect of faith: first, as an act of the intellect initiated by the will, which drives the intellect to a new field of knowledge and thus provides the intellect with a new basis for cognition;[126] and second, as an acquired faith, which is not a product of man's own mind but comes from the outside, a gift from God.[127] Luther, Calvin, and Zwingli, rejecting the former concept of faith, lacked that certain level of responsibility placed by the Anabaptist reformer on man's need to respond to God's work, made possible through his trichotomous anthropology.[128] In regard to salvation, therefore, Steinmetz accurately concludes that "whereas Zwingli emphasized divine initiative and the freedom of the Holy Spirit, Hubmaier stressed the human response to grace and the freedom of the will."[129] This response of man is, in turn, brought about, at least in its initial stage, through the preaching of the Word. Faith, then, comes from God as one responds to the Word preached by his messengers.[130]

THE IMPORT OF CHURCH DISCIPLINE TO HUBMAIER'S ANTHROPOLOGY

As relates to the Radical Reformer's anthropological understanding, the trichotomous division of the nature of man is what propels Hubmaier to esteem the doctrine of church discipline so highly. First, man's freedom of the will, made possible by Hubmaier's anthropology, plays an important role in the voluntary nature of church membership. Hubmaier's anthropological position moved him to assert that the church could and

---

126. Oberman, *The Harvest of Medieval Theology*, 70; Biel, *Epitome*, III.23.2.I.I.C.

127. Oberman, *The Harvest of Medieval Theology*, 71; Biel, *Epitome*, III.23.2.2.I. In this same section, Biel also mentioned infused faith, although he did not believe it to be a necessity, but helpful to strengthen and perfect the act of faith.

128. It is the spirit's retention of the pre-fall wholeness that enables man in the first place to respond to the preached word. This concept is reminiscent of the Medieval idea of *synderesis*, discussed by Biel and covered earlier in the chapter.

129. Steinmetz, "Nominalist Motifs in Hubmaier," 130. See also Hall, "Erasmian Influence".

130. "Daneben findet Hubmaier in der Apostelgeschichte sowie in den synoptischen Belegen zur Taufe die unaufgebbare und verbindliche Ordnung von Predigt—Glaube—Taufe. Der dem Menschen vorgeschriebene Weg zum Heil beginnt mit dem Hören des Wortes Gottes in der Predigt." Windhorst, *Täferisches Taufverständnis*, 193.

must be a voluntary community of believers. Choosing to believe and obtaining salvation solely by God's grace, men are then able to enter into a new covenant with God through believer's baptism. The process of water baptism further involves the voluntary permission given to one's fellow believers to be disciplined by them through fraternal admonition or the ban, should the need for that ever arise.

Second, Hubmaier's anthropology, with the help of his doctrine of church discipline, enables him, in the words of Friedmann, to "answer the problem of human existence in the affirmative."[131] While Friedmann's statement evaluates the anthropology of the Anabaptists in general, it certainly fits well Hubmaier's understanding of the doctrine of man and its correlation with church discipline: "As man receives grace a new life arises in his heart and makes him ready to be a follower of Christ, and as such to be a lover of his neighbor and a brother to his fellow believer. By this he also conquers, at least to a certain extent, the sinful urge in his soul. Anthropology thus assumes a new aspect and answers the problem of human existence in the affirmative."[132]

This "being a brother to his fellow believer" takes place through keeping one another accountable through the process of church discipline. The key theological element, therefore, that enables Anabaptist anthropology in general, and Hubmaier's in particular, to "answer the problem of human existence in the affirmative" is brotherly admonition or church discipline, according to Friedmann's assessment.

Third, it is because human beings consist of three parts, one of which was unaffected by the fall and remains free to choose, that the Waldshut priest is able to keep a perfect tension between the church's ability to execute eternal judgments on the erring sinners and the believer's ability to retain his salvation. For it is the flesh, Hubmaier believes, that is being punished by the church in the case of a ban, so that, even in the worst case scenario of an unrepentent miscreant, his body may be committed to Satan for destruction, while his spirit, the incorruptible part of him, would be preserved and saved. The Anabaptist reformer clearly states this idea in his exegesis of the 1 Cor 5 passage: "in our congregation we . . .

---

131. Friedmann, *The Theology of Anabaptism*, 174.
132. Ibid., 74.

Church Discipline and Anthropology 53

give you over to the devil for the destruction of the flesh so that the spirit might be saved on the day of the Lord Jesus."[133]

In *Freedom of the Will, I*, Hubmaier revisits the 1 Cor 5 scenario and reiterates his understanding of the important role of church discipline in relation to the spirit's condition when he writes in the following:

> In the same way also, so that the spirit might be saved, Paul gives the fornicator to the devil for the destruction of the flesh in the power of our Lord Jesus Christ, that is, in the power of the keys, which Christ has given to his bride, the Christian church, to bind and to loose on earth after him, 1 Cor 5:5; Matt 16:19; 18:18; John 20:23. It is as if he were to say, "If the flesh wants to be ruined and of the devil, then we give it to him; but the spirit remains saved and whole for the day of the Lord."[134]

This is a perfect illustration of the way that the doctrine of church discipline enables the Waldshut reformer to keep his anthropological edifice together. For it is in the judgment and the condemnation of the flesh to the devil, an act of church discipline to be exercised by the congregation, that the spirit is able to keep its salvation and wholeness until the Lord's Day. Ryan Klassen converges with this interpretation of Hubmaier's anthropology when he writes that "Salvation is still a possibility for those outside the Church (the excommunicated or unevangelized) but not while they remain alive on earth."[135]

Having examined Balthasar Hubmaier's understanding of the doctrine of man, the task of the next chapter will be to assess the way that man can re-establish his relationship with God. Thus Hubmaier's soteriology will be under close scrutiny, involving his views of justification and sanctification.

---

133. Hubmaier, "Ban," 417; Hubmaier, "Schriften," 372.

134. Hubmaier, "Freedom, I," 434–35; Hubmaier, "Schriften," 386.

135. Klassen, "Two Swords," 65. In the age in which we now live, salvation can only be obtained within the church. Upon Christ's return, He will evaluate the church's decisions with regard to confirming and denying salvation to individuals on this earth. Some of the church's decisions will be ratified, others will be modified. It is in this context that Klassen's understanding of Hubmaier must be read.

3

Church Discipline and Soteriology

INTRODUCTION TO THE SIXTEENTH-CENTURY DOCTRINE OF SALVATION

THE TURBULENT YEARS OF the sixteenth century thrust the doctrine of salvation to a place of utmost import in the contemporaneous theological development. The rise of various schools of theology in the Middle Ages, outlined in the previous chapter, resulted in doctrinal pluralism at the top of the theological echelons, which, for the average believer, translated into nothing more than doctrinal confusion. The doctrine of salvation seemed to suffer the most from this confusion.

The Catholic Church had no simple answer to the question of what one must do to be saved. According to Alister E. McGrath, there were several factors contributing to this confusion. First, there had been no authoritative pronouncement from the Roman church on the matter for over a thousand years.[1] In 418, the Council of Carthage briefly discussed the question and in 529, the Second Council of Orange outlined more detailed soteriological proposals. For a reason unknown, the theologians of the Middle Ages, however, were unaware of the latter council's decisions until 1546. By the time that the soteriological proposals of the Council of

---

1. McGrath, *Reformation Thought*, 91.

Orange had been rediscovered, as McGrath notes, "the Reformation had been under way for a generation."[2]

Second, since the doctrine of salvation seems to have been a favorite topic of debate among later medieval theologians, "a disproportionately large number of opinions on the question passed into circulation."[3] The Catholic Church's unwillingness or inability to evaluate these different views ensured complete confusion on the part of the average believer. This made the perfect environment for the Reformation movement of the sixteenth century. While the Reformation is often portrayed as a rediscovery of the Bible, and particularly of the Pauline corpus, in McGrath's befitting estimation, it is "considerably more accurate to portray it as a rediscovery of Augustine's doctrine of grace, with a subsequent critique of his doctrine of the church."[4]

An accurate placement of Balthasar Hubmaier's soteriology, therefore, is only possible when his understanding of salvation is considered against the larger context of the time in which he lived and the prevailing theological movements of the day. The previous chapter demonstrated Hubmaier's theological convergence with the late medieval scholasticism, Augustinianism, and Erasmus' humanism. This chapter will establish the fact of his indebtedness, at least early on, to the soteriological understanding of Martin Luther and the Magisterial Reformers. Above all, however, it must be remembered that Hubmaier aspired to be a biblical theologian.[5]

Although the subject of Luther's influence upon Hubmaier was already broached in chapter 1, the current topic necessitates a more detailed focus on this issue. As such, the doctrine of salvation propagated by Martin Luther and that of the Reformed branch, represented by John Calvin, demands consideration next as a segueway to Hubmaier's own soteriology.

Luther's Understanding of Salvation

Martin Luther's personal experience of conversion, which formed a solid foundation for his understanding of soteriology, was a result of the

---

2. Ibid.
3. Ibid.
4. McGrath, *Iustitia Dei*, 189.
5. Estep, "Anabaptist View," 35.

threefold realization: first, no works could satisfy God's wrath; second, God's righteousness was unattainable to humans bound in sin; and third, one could only be saved by grace alone. In fact, the question of how sinners are justified, in the words of Alister E. McGrath, was "at the heart of Luther's Reforming programme."[6]

In 1545, the year before he died, Luther wrote a preface to the first volume of the complete edition of his Latin writings in order to describe how he parted ways with the Catholic Church.[7] In the preface Luther introduced his personal struggle with the "righteousness of God" and related his conversion in the following words:

> I had certainly wanted to understand Paul in his letter to the Romans. But what prevented me from doing so was not so much cold feet as that one phrase in the first chapter: "the righteousness of God is revealed in it" (Rom 1:17). For I hated that phrase, "the righteousness of God," which I had been taught to understand as the righteousness by which God is righteous, and punishes unrighteous sinners.
>
> Although I lived a blameless life as a monk, I felt that I was a sinner with an uneasy conscience before God. I also could not believe that I had pleased him with my works. Far from loving that righteous God who punished sinners, I actually hated him . . . I was in desperation to know what Paul meant in this passage. At last, as I meditated day and night on the relation of the words "the righteousness of God is revealed in it, as it is written, the righteous person shall live by faith," I began to understand that "righteousness of God" as that by which the righteous person lives by the gift of God (faith); and this sentence, "the righteousness of God is revealed," to refer to a passive righteousness, by which the merciful God justifies us by faith.[8]

Emir Caner's summary of Luther's progress in soteriological understanding is accurate: "Through his own personal experience, Luther had changed his mind from a salvation based on human works to that based

---

6. McGrath, *Reformation Thought*, 88.

7. Ibid., 95.

8. The full text of Luther's quotation may be found in Luther, *Luther's Works, Vol.34*, 95. The present quotation was somewhat paraphrased and abridged by Alister E. McGrath, who omitted some of Luther's more technical phrases for the sake of clarity, McGrath, *Reformation Thought*, 95.

Church Discipline and Soteriology

solely on the finished work of Christ."[9] By the virtue of his education at the University of Erfurt, it is safe to assume that Luther's previous understanding of the basis of salvation was in line with the school's official position on the subject, that of the *via moderna*.[10] In accordance with the *via moderna*'s teaching, in Luther's early understanding of salvation, God made a covenant with humanity, according to which all who humble themselves before God can expect to be justified as a matter of course.[11] Concomitant with the *via moderna*'s concept, "the covenant between God and humanity established a framework within which a relatively small human effort," which is required to place God under an obligation to reward the sinner with grace, "results in a disproportionately large divine reward."[12]

Between 1514 and 1519, however, for reasons which may never be known, Luther's understanding of salvation and in particular justification underwent a serious transformation. The impetus for this alteration was brought about by his personal struggle with the idea of the righteousness of God, which he understood to refer to an impartial divine attribute.[13] McGrath summarizes aptly the concept of God's righteousness which became so bothersome for the reformer: "God judges individuals with complete impartiality. If the individual has met the basic precondition for justification, he or she is justified; if he has not, he or she is condemned. God shows neither leniency nor favouritism: he judges solely on the basis of merit. God is both equitable and just, in that he gives each individual exactly what he or she merits—nothing more and nothing less."[14]

A closer study of Augustine convinced Luther that a depraved humanity was too corrupt for man to be able to initiate the process of salvation.[15] Because of this, "the righteousness of God" became a condemning factor that haunted the reformer day and night. With the help of the writings of Augustine, however, Luther came to realize that the whole process of salvation, from its initiation, when faith is granted by God as

---

9. Caner, "Balthasar Hubmaier: Life and Writings," 196.

10. For a more thorough discussion of the *via moderna* ideas relevant to this research, see the section on Scholasticism in Chapter 2.

11. Luther, *Luther's Works*, Vol. 10, 235–43.

12. McGrath, *Reformation Thought*, 93.

13. McGrath, *Iustitia Dei*, 190–97. See also McGrath, *Reformation Thought*, 93–97.

14. McGrath, *Reformation Thought*, 93.

15. Luther, *Luther's Works*, Vol. 34, 155, 185–87.

a precondition to salvation, to the end of sanctification and glorification, was the work of God.[16] It was initiated, instituted, and enabled by God alone, with absolutely no human participation. This later understanding of Luther's is expressed well in his Commentary on Galatians, based on the 1531 lectures on the book. In commenting on chapter 5 verse 4, in his *Lectures on Galatians*, Luther writes, "For Christ alone justifies me, in opposition to my evil works and without my good works."[17]

Thus justification by faith alone, where even faith itself was a gift from God, became the battle cry of the Wittenberg reformer. Luther's understanding of faith, therefore, as aforementioned, came from Pauline theology viewed through the lens of Augustine. Luther's regard for Augustine is not surprising, for the rise in interest in Augustinian studies, identified by McGrath as "an aspect of the Renaissance in general," was characteristic of the age in which the Wittenberg reformer lived.[18] As such, to find that Luther's idea of even faith itself being God's gift was found in Augustine's writings first, is not unusual.[19] What was unquestionably new and different about Luther's interaction with Augustine, as opposed to that of his contemporaries, was the use to which he put the earlier church father's doctrine.[20]

The concept of justification by faith alone evolved into another important soteriological aspect shared by all the Magisterial Reformers, namely that of forensic justification.[21] According to the notion of forensic justification, God considers a sinner righteous on account of his righteousness, which originates and remains outside the sinner. Luther's concept of forensic justification signaled a break from the established Augustinian

---

16. Ibid., 246.
17. Ibid., 17.
18. McGrath, *Iustitia Dei*, 189.
19. Augustine, "On Grace and Free Will," I.17, 28: "His last clause runs thus: 'I have kept the faith.' But he who says this is the same who declares in another passage, 'I have obtained mercy that I might be faithful.' He does not say, 'I obtained mercy because I was faithful,' but 'in order that I might be faithful,' thus showing that even faith itself cannot be had without God's mercy, and that it is the gift of God. This he very expressly teaches us when he says, 'For by grace are ye saved through faith, and not of yourselves; it is the gift of God.'" "Both alike are therefore due to the grace of God,—the faith of those who believe, and the patience of those who suffer, because the apostle spoke of both as *given* [emphasis present]."
20. McGrath, *Iustitia Dei*, 189.
21. McGrath, *Reformation Thought*, 106–8.

model of God's impartation of His righteousness to the believer as the grounds for his justification. Contrary to Augustine, Luther held that believers are righteous on account of the alien righteousness of Christ which is imputed rather than imparted to them—that is they are treated as if righteousness were theirs through faith. This criterion, according to McGrath, namely extrinsic versus intrinsic nature of justifying righteousness, "served to distinguish the doctrines of justification associated with the Magisterial Reformation from those of Catholicism on one hand, and the Radical Reformation on the other."[22]

Reformed Understanding of Salvation

Though Hubmaier's interaction with the Reformed understanding of salvation came mainly through the person and writings of Ulrich Zwingli, the prolific nature and wide accessibility of the writings of the Genevan Reformer, John Calvin, make him a better contender for the present consideration. John Calvin's model of justification was formulated in the 1540s and 1550s. If "justification by faith alone" was the distinguishing factor of Luther's reformation, then "justification through predetermined grace" was the main feature of Zwingli and Calvin's reformation, and by extension, of the Reformed movement. In his *Institutes of the Christian Religion*, Calvin described justification in the following way: "grace is predestined to those to whom the possession of glory was previously assigned the Lord being pleased to bring his sons by election to justification."[23]

Faith, according to Calvin, unites the believer to Christ in a "mystic union."[24] Much like in Luther's theology, it was in Christ that the believer has access to the alien righteousness of Christ, which alone is to be credited for his justification and regeneration. This union with Christ, the backbone of Calvin's theology, has a twofold effect to which the reformer refers as "double grace." First, the believer's union with Christ leads directly to his justification:

> Scripture, when it treats of justification by faith . . . bids us look only to the mercy of God and the perfection of Christ. The order of justification which it sets before us is this: first, God of his mere gratuitous goodness is pleased to embrace the sinner, in whom

22. McGrath, *Iustitia Dei*, 190.
23. John Calvin, *Institutes of the Christian Religion*, 3.22.9.
24. McGrath, *Reformation Thought*, 112.

he sees nothing that can move him to mercy but wretchedness, because he sees him altogether naked and destitute of good works. He, therefore, seeks the cause of kindness in himself, that thus he may affect the sinner by a sense of his goodness, and induce him, in distrust of his own works, to cast himself entirely upon his mercy for salvation. This is the meaning of faith by which the sinner comes into the possession of salvation, when, according to the doctrine of the Gospel, he perceives that he is reconciled by God; when, by the intercession of Christ, he obtains the pardon of his sins, and is justified; and, though renewed by the Spirit of God, considers that, instead of leaning on his own works, he must look solely to the righteousness which is treasured up for him in Christ.[25]

Second, on account of the believer's union with Christ, and not on account of his justification, the believer begins the process of becoming like Christ through regeneration. Both are the results of the believer's union with Christ through faith.[26]

HUBMAIER'S SOTERIOLOGY

According to Harold S. Bender, "the Anabaptist doctrine of regeneration and discipleship was expressed in the context of Reformation theology and practice, and in conscious opposition to it."[27] This description of the Anabaptist soteriology is certainly inclusive of Hubmaier's understanding of salvation. "According to Hubmaier," in the words of Eddie L. Mabry, "God's activity of grace, by which He justifies fallen humanity, is the process, and salvation is the ultimate goal of this process."[28] Salvation for Balthasar Hubmaier, therefore, is a process in which fallen humans are reconciled to God not by virtue of God declaring them righteous, as with the Magisterial Reformers, but through an actual transformation, upon which they become acceptable to Him.[29] In other words, "acceptance before God (or justification), for Hubmaier, is not a forensic announcement of such by God concerning one who is not really a saint; but, rather, it is

25. Calvin, *Institutes*, 3.11.16.
26. McGrath, *Reformation Thought*, 112.
27. Bender, "Walking in the Resurrection," 102.
28. Mabry, *Doctrine of the Church*, 102.
29. MacGregor, *European Synthesis*, 114.

Church Discipline and Soteriology 61

God's acceptance of a righteousness that is actually present, and that is made possible by one's restoration and the ability to reach perfect righteousness through grace."[30]

The salvific process in the Radical Reformer's theology commences "with an inner regeneration experience . . . at the moment when a person appropriately responds to God's Word," and "continues under the shepherding of the church until she or he is converted into a totally righteous person."[31] Although their language may have portrayed otherwise, neither Hubmaier, nor the majority of the Anabaptists ever taught that it was possible for believers to reach perfection here on earth. The ardent commitment to the practice of church discipline in their congregations provides perhaps the strongest proof of that. Hubmaier explains in his own words his understanding of salvation:

> On the order of Christian justification: when a person now confesses himself to be a sinner, believes on the forgiveness of sins, and has committed himself to a new life, then he professes this also outwardly and publicly before the Christian church, into whose fellowship he lets himself be registered and counted according to the order and institution of Christ. Therefore he professes to the Christian church, that is, to all brothers and sisters who live in faith, that in his heart he has been thus inwardly instructed in the Word of Christ and so minded that he has surrendered himself already to live according to the Word, will, and Rule of Christ, to arrange and direct his doing and not doing according to him, and also to fight and strive under his banner until death . . . The flesh must daily be killed since it wants only to live and reign according to its own lusts. Here the Spirit of Christ prevails and gains the victory. Then the person brings forth good fruits which give testimony of a good tree. Day and night he practices all those things which concern the praise of God and brotherly love. By this the old Adam is martyred, killed, and carried to the grave. This is a summary and right order of a whole Christian life which begins in the Word of God.[32]

As is evident from Hubmaier's statement above, as well as his explicit pronouncement of the fact, the Anabaptist leader agreed with the

---

30. Mabry, *Doctrine of the Church*, 109.

31. MacGregor, *European Synthesis*, 114.

32. Hubmaier, "Christian Baptism," 143, 145, 147; Hubmaier, "Schriften," 157, 160–61.

common understanding of medieval theology, dating all the way back to Cyprian, that there is no salvation outside of the church. While for the medieval church, however, this was true "because only in the church were the sacraments that were necessary for salvation properly administered and received," Hubmaier believed it to be so because of the church's "instructional and shepherding role, which Christ has given only to the church with the investiture of the keys."[33] Eddie Mabry further elaborates on the church's significant role in Hubmaier's understanding of the salvific process: "while the inner regeneration process must take place before one is incorporated into the church; it is, nevertheless, through the church that one hears the Word, or the gospel, that leads to regeneration, and it is within the church that one receives the nurturing necessary for the continuous process of justification."[34] Writing half of century ago, Robert Friedmann's comments contrasting the present Protestant view of salvation as individualistic transaction to that of Anabaptist concept of the sixteenth century are still especially helpful in grasping the important role that the church played in Hubmaier's soteriological understanding:

> Everybody still remains alone, seeking his personal salvation, and he only enjoys the sharing of edification with the like minded coreligionists. Or to put it in other words: the brother is not absolutely necessary for the salvation of the individual, which rests alone in the possession of one's faith. It is but one further step from this position to the liberal concept of individualism of the last hundred years, [which] almost atomized society and destroyed church life at large . . .
>
> Now then, the central idea of Anabaptism, the real dynamite in the age of Reformation, as I see it, was this, that one cannot find salvation without caring for his brother, that this "brother" actually matters in the personal life . . . This interdependence of men gives life and salvation a new meaning. It is not "faith alone" which matters (for which faith no church organization would be needed) but it is brotherhood, this intimate caring for each other, as it was commanded to the disciples of Christ as the way to God's kingdom. That was the discovery which made Anabaptism so forceful and outstanding in all of church history.[35]

---

33. Mabry, *Doctrine of the Church*, 101.

34. Ibid., 102.

35. Friedmann, "On Mennonite Historiography and on Individualism and Brotherhood," 121.

Church Discipline and Soteriology 63

What enabled the church to fulfill its momentous role in the process of one's salvation was its utilization of church discipline. Thus from the very outset of considering Hubmaier's soteriology, it is evident that his doctrine of church discipline plays an especially prominent role in this area of his theology.

Considering the import of the doctrine of salvation to the theological debates of the sixteenth century, it seems peculiar that Hubmaier did not develop this doctrine anywhere in his writings in a separate and systematic manner, "even where we might fairly expect to find it—in his catechism," notes Henry C. Vedder in his book, *Balthasar Hubmaier: The Leader of the Anabaptists*.[36] The reason for such a strange omission, according to Vedder, could have been because the Anabaptist preacher was trying to disassociate himself from Luther's concept of this principle.[37] In spite of the absence of separate and systematic treatment of the doctrine of salvation within the writings of Hubmaier, there is sufficient material pertaining to this doctrine interspersed throughout his treatises. In the following pages the task of this manuscript will be to reconstruct the Radical Reformer's understanding of salvation from his own writings. In the process, as aforementioned, the doctrine of church discipline will emerge as an essential part of Hubmaier's soteriology, without which the preacher of Waldshut might not have been able to make the latter come together.

Hubmaier's Understanding of Justification

"The Anabaptists accepted the Lutheran formula of justification by faith," writes Robert Kreider, "but they insisted that this faith must be evidenced (*Bussfertigkeit*) by newness of character."[38] Balthasar Hubmaier makes the former idea clear in the first of his *Eighteen Theses*: "Faith alone makes us righteous (*fromm*) before God."[39] Hubmaier articulates the latter idea in equally clear terms in the third thesis: "Such faith cannot be idle, but must break forth (*außbrechen*) in gratitude toward God and in all sorts of works of brotherly love toward others."[40] This "breaking forth in grati-

---

36. Vedder, *Hübmaier*, 200–201.
37. Ibid., 201.
38. Kreider, "Anabaptism and Humanism," 138.
39. Hubmaier, "Eighteen Theses," 32; Hubmaier, "Schriften," 72.
40. Hubmaier, "Eighteen Theses," 32; Hubmaier, "Schriften," 72.

tude" was otherwise known among the Anabaptists as *Nachfolge Christi*, "discipleship following Christ."

Thus Hubmaier did not seem to create a dichotomy between salvation and discipleship; those who were saved would desire to and, in fact, work out their salvation by means of these "works of brotherly love." The "works of brotherly love," in Hubmaier's words, or "works of faith," in the words of Hans Jürgen-Goertz, "were incorporated into the process of justification."[41] Professor von Muralt's summary of the teaching of the Swiss Brethren describes perfectly Hubmaier's understanding of the relationship between faith and "works of brotherly love": "Faith and transformation of life stand in the most intimate connection for the Anabaptists. Faith produces the transformation; I would say, faith is the reality, faith takes form in the transformation, or even closer, faith is transformation of life. The Anabaptists teach the obedience of faith."[42]

Similarly, Harold S. Bender's masterful description of the wholistic nature of the Anabaptist idea of discipleship serves to broaden the reader's understanding of the immediate context of Hubmaier's thought on the subject:

> deeply characteristic of the Anabaptist theology of discipleship [was] the inseparability of belief and practice, faith and life. To profess a new birth meant a new life. To take the name of Christ meant to take His spirit and His nature. To promise obedience to Him meant actually to live out and carry through His principles and do His works... To be a disciple meant to teach and to observe all things whatsoever the Master had taught and commanded.
>
> This absolute disciples applied to all areas of life. It meant a church composed only of disciples, not a mixture of disciples and worldlings.[43]

In other words, in sync with his Anabaptist contemporaries, Hubmaier taught that fruits of faith, that is, works of obedience, are not just the *result* of saving faith, but belong to the *essence* of saving

---

41. Jürgen-Goertz, *Anabaptists*, 63.

42. "Glaube und Umwandlung des Menschen stehen bei den Täufern im engsten Zusammenhang. Der Glaube wirkt die Umwandlung, ich möchte sagen, der Glaube wird Wirklichkeit, der Glaube wird Gestalt in der Umwandlung, oder noch enger, der Glaube ist Umwandlung des Menschen." Muralt, *Glaube und Lehre*, 35.

43. Bender, "The Anabaptist Theology of Discipleship," 31.

Church Discipline and Soteriology 65

faith.[44] According to Bender's article "'Walking in the Resurrection': The Anabaptist Doctrine of Regeneration and Discipleship," the title of which was borrowed from a phrase in the Schleitheim Confession, the Anabaptists' "sound understanding of the gospel as promising victory in the struggle with sin, and as making possible the life of love and good works," was what lay at the foundation of their "vigorous emphasis . . . upon holy living and discipleship as the fruit of regeneration."[45]

Hubmaier and the Anabaptists, therefore, neither held to a works-righteousness nor were motivated by a desire for sanctification as merely a divine gift.[46] They held instead, according to Cornelius J. Dyck, "to the notion of discipleship, of following simply out of love for Jesus and respect for the command of Scripture. Obedience was first of all a response of gratitude and identification with Christ."[47] Given this understanding of justification and sanctification, "the redemptive function of church discipline becomes obvious."[48] The practice of church discipline through correction aided the believers in maintaining their loving obedience to Christ.

Even Hubmaier's choice of vocabulary identifies the uniqueness of his soteriology. It is of interest, for example that "in Hubmaier's writings there is no mention of the word 'justification' (*Rechfertigung*)."[49] Rather than using the common German term *Rechfertigung* for justification, Hubmaier utilizes the root word "*fromm*." This word in German usually means "pious," or "devout." Although *Rechfertigung* and *fromm* could be and were used interchangeably by various German theologians of his time, it is the exclusivity of the Anabaptist leader's usage of *fromm* that is of significance. The reason for the exclusive usage of *fromm*, as aptly elucidated by Mabry, is this: "Justification for Hubmaier, . . . means something closer to *Gerechtmachung* (making right or just); rather than the usual Lutheran forensic sense of justification, as being, acceptable before God as if one were just."[50]

44. Ludwig, "Sanctification and Discipline," 82.
45. Bender, "Walking in the Resurrection," 101.
46. Ludwig, "Sanctification and Discipline," 82.
47. Dyck, "Life of the Spirit in Anabaptism," 317.
48. Ludwig, "Sanctification and Discipline," 82.
49. Mabry, *Doctrine of the Church*, 103.
50. Ibid., 103. Additionally, while the Magisterial Reformers also used *Frombmachung*, for them it entailed a forensic change in status before God rather than ontological change

The aforementioned theological terms shaped the way that Hubmaier translated and interpreted Scripture in his sermons from 1523 onward.[51] Fluent in Greek and often using Erasmus' *Greek New Testament*, Hubmaier always rendered as much of it in the vernacular as was possible. Preaching on 1 Tim 1:15, which notes that Christ came into the world "to save sinners," where the Greek text had *hamartōlous sōsai* and the *Vulgate—peccatores salvos facere*, Hubmaier translated this phrase as *den sünder gerecht vnd fromb zemachen*, meaning "to make aright and just or pious,"[52] thus equating personal holiness with the condition of salvation.[53] A similar phenomenon can be observed in Hubmaier's translation of Rom 4:25 in his *On the Christian Baptism of Believers*. The passage relates Christ's death and resurrection as being "for our justification," with Greek text stating *dia tēn dikaiōsin hēmōn* and Latin—*propter justificationem nostram*, which Hubmaier again translates as "*von vnserer frommachung*."[54] Later in the same treatise, under the section entitled "Von der ordnung einer christlichen frombmachung,"[55] Hubmaier writes, "your physician, who came into this world to make sinners righteous and God-fearing (or justified)."[56] Here, "justified" is expressed with the German word *fromm*. Later in the same treatise, Hubmaier uses the term *Gesundmachung*, revealing to his readers that in his mind being made healthy and justification are synonymous concepts: "Through such words of comfort the sinner is enlivened again, comes to himself, becomes joyful and henceforth surrenders himself entirely to this physician Christ. All his sickness he commits, submits, and entrusts to him. As much as it is possible for a wounded person he will also surrender to the will of the Lord. He calls upon him daily for healing and purification."[57]

---

promoted by Hubmaier.

51. MacGregor, *European Synthesis*, 116.

52. Hubmaier, "Summa," 84; Hubmaier, "Schriften," 111.

53. MacGregor, *European Synthesis*, 116. See also Windhorst, *Täferisches Taufverständnis*, 25–26.

54. Hubmaier, "Christian Baptism," 115; Hubmaier, "Schriften," 134.

55. "The Order of Christian Justification."

56 . Hubmaier, "Christian Baptism," 144; "eüwer artzt sey, der kummen ist inn dise welt, den sünder gerecht vnd fromb zumachen," Hubmaier, "Schriften," 159.

57. Hubmaier, "Christian Baptism," 144; Hubmaier, "Schriften," 159.

As Hans Jürgen-Goertz points out, Hubmaier "regarded the notion that salvation came from faith alone and not from works as an excuse to continue living a wicked life."[58]

An awareness of the reformer's distinctive anthropology, unveiled in the previous chapter, allows one to understand better his soteriology. Due to the fallen state of humanity brought about by Adam's sin, a rebirth was necessary if salvation was to occur:

> Now we surely know that originally God made all things good and especially the human being in spirit, soul, and body. However, by the disobedience of Adam this goodness in us has been wounded in the soul, it has been held captive and obscured in the spirit by the darkness of the body, and has been completely ruined in the flesh. If we would again be free in the spirit, be healed in the soul, and also that this Fall be unharmful to us in the flesh, then such must, must, must take place through a new birth, as Christ himself says, or we will not enter into the Kingdom of God.[59]

This rebirth for Hubmaier is an actual ontological transformation accomplished by the means of grace. "Through the transformed and new condition of health and wholeness," summarizes Mabry, "and the living of the saintly life, one was justified."[60] Therefore, salvation, in the mind of the Waldshut reformer, is a process by which fallen humans are reconciled to God, through which the sinner is recreated and actually made right and acceptable, rather than just considered it, in the sight of God.[61] Thus, unlike the Magisterial Reformers, whose forensic justification carried the idea of a change in status before God rather than a change in the person's essential nature, Hubmaier believes there is an actual change in one's basic condition. In this sense of justification, as Mabry aptly delineates, the sinner is not simply accepted as if whole; he is actually made whole in his essential nature: "*Frombmachung* therefore was not simply something which God graciously announced to one who accepted in faith what Christ had done; but, rather, it was an actual change in the nature of the person. The soul of the fallen was restored to its originally created condition, and the person was restored to health. When Hubmaier used the term *fromm* or *Frombmachung* to translate the *Vulgate* term *justus*,

---

58. Jürgen-Goertz, *Anabaptists*, 63.
59. Hubmaier, "Ban," 445; Hubmaier, "Schriften," 395.
60. Mabry, *Doctrine of the Church*, 107.
61 . Ibid., 101; Hubmaier, "Christian Baptism," 144–45; Hubmaier, "Schriften," 159.

therefore, it was with the idea of an essential transformation of the nature of the person."[62]

This being made healthy, being transformed to wholeness or justification, is a process that takes place in two stages. The first stage is one's restoration to the originally created purity and goodness through the death of Christ.[63] Because of the universal sense in which this restoration was accomplished, men could participate in justification by exercising faith as initial belief.[64] As Hubmaier stated, "God has created you without your help, but without your help he will not save you."[65] While some have been and may be tempted to interpret this statement of the reformer as referring to works-based salvation, a word of caution may be in order here. For, considering the context of the statement, Hubmaier's intent is to communicate the necessity of one's exercising faith as a prerequisite to salvation. In other words, God is not going to save someone who either does not desire it or does not believe in him. This participation on the man's part, in fact, is quite important for Hubmaier's salvific transaction to be made complete. Alvin J. Beachy notes similarly in his work *The Concept of Grace in the Radical Reformation*: "Thus Hubmaier, in his development of a doctrine of the freedom of the will, shows concern not only for man's moral responsibility but also for the personal and voluntary character of Christian salvation with the implication that compulsion would be a violation of grace and for the protection of the moral character of God."[66]

Hubmaier's particular understanding of human participation in the act of salvation was partially affected by his literal understanding of Rom 2:13, "For it is not those who hear the commandments that are righteous before God, but those who fulfill the law that will be justified."[67] Another passage that contributed to the reformer's soteriological comprehension was James 2:14-19, according to which Hubmaier wrote that "mere faith does not deserve to be called faith, for a true faith can never exist without deeds of love."[68] Rollin Armour correctly observes: "Without that brief

---

62. Mabry, *Doctrine of the Church*, 106.

63. Ibid., 107.

64. Hubmaier, "Freedom, I," 443; Hubmaier, "Schriften," 393.

65. Hubmaier, "Freedom, I," 440; Hubmaier, "Schriften," 391.

66. Beachy, *Grace in the Radical Reformation*, 53.

67. Hubmaier, "Freedom of the Will, II," 490; Hubmaier, "Schriften," 430.

68 . Hubmaier, "Apologia," 527; Hubmaier, "Schriften," 462. If this statement sounds too much like the Catholic doctrine of salvation, it is due to the fact that it was penned on

Church Discipline and Soteriology 69

moment of personal commitment following the hearing of the Gospel and preceding the full regenerating gift of grace, there could be, in Hubmaier's view, neither personal conversion nor objective grounds for baptism."[69]

The first stage of justification is necessary to the reformer's theology due to his desire to depict humans as not being completely under bondage to sin, but as having the natural capacity to will and to do good, and therefore to respond with spontaneous faith to God's call for repentance.[70] Since the fall destroyed the soul's ability to distinguish between right and wrong, as pointed out in the previous chapter, the restoration to the original condition is integral to Hubmaier's theology as a whole.

The Radical Reformer would be quick to admit, however, that first, even this human participation is made possible by God, who alone initiates and makes possible the whole process in the beginning.[71] Eddie Mabry emphasizes this point quite effectively: "It is God who has mercy on the fallen condition. When fallen individuals can do nothing for themselves, it is God who sends His Son as a gift of grace, to die for sins, through which they may be restored to original health again. It is God who effects the second sending of the Word, with justifying (or saving) faith. Justification therefore is something that God effects out of boundless mercy."[72]

Second, in Hubmaier's initial stage of justification, this participation on the part of men did not instigate the salvific process. God was the originator and his grace enabled men to respond to his Word in initial belief, which was rewarded with justifying faith.[73] Justification, therefore, is essentially the work of God that he effects out of his boundless mercy.[74]

The second stage of justification involves the second sending of the Word, namely the preached Word, enlivened by the Holy Spirit, revealing

---

January 3, 1528 from Kreuzenstein prison as an attempt to appease his Catholic captors and gain a release from bonds. As such, considering the surrounding circumstances, it is difficult to know how much weight can be ascribed to this statement and whether Hubmaier really meant it.

69. Armour, *Anabaptist Baptism*, 31.
70. Mabry, *Doctrine of the Church*, 108.
71. Hubmaier, "Freedom, I," 439; Hubmaier, "Schriften," 390.
72. Mabry, *Doctrine of the Church*, 107–08.
73. Hubmaier, "Freedom, I," 439–40, 444; Hubmaier, "Schriften," 390, 394.
74. Mabry, *Doctrine of the Church*, 108.

to man his sinfulness.[75] This revelation, without which one could not know the depths of one's depravity, causes man to respond with initial belief. God rewards this response with justifying faith, giving man the power to do what he commands: "For the divine Word is so powerful, authoritative, and strong in the believers that the person (though not the godless one) can will and do everything that said Word commands him to want and to do."[76] In writing these words, Hubmaier not only affirms the power of God's Word but also indirectly accuses the Magisterial Reformers of having a false dichotomy between God's call to salvation and man's utter inability to heed the call.

Hubmaier illustrated the two stages of justification with his analogy of the Good Samaritan's application of wine and oil to the wounds of the sinner:

> Then the Samaritan must come, that is, Christ Jesus. He brings along medicine, namely, wine and oil, which he pours into the wounds of the sinner. Wine: he leads the person to repentance so that he is sorry for his sins. He brings oil, by which he softens his pain and drives it away, and says, "Believe the gospel that clearly shows that I am your physician who has come into this world to make the sinner just and righteous . . . Through such words of comfort the sinner is enlivened again, comes to himself, becomes joyful, and henceforth surrenders himself entirely to the physician . . . As much as it is possible for a wounded person he will also surrender to the will of the physician. He calls upon him for healing so that what the wounded is not able to do out of his own capacity, the physician counsels, helps, and promotes him so that he can follow his Word and commandment.[77]

To recapitulate, Hubmaier's *ordo salutis*, as catalogued by Beachy using the Radical's *On the Christian Baptism of Believers*, is as follows:

> First, one must be led through the Word of God to a knowledge of his sins, and he must confess that he is a sinner. Second, one must be taught again by the Word of God that he should cry to God, the Father, for the forgiveness of his sins for Christ's sake. Third, where one now does this in faith and does not doubt, God cleanses his heart in faith and trust and forgives him all his sins. After one experiences this grace and goodness, he gives himself to God and

---

75. Windhorst, *Täferisches Taufverständnis*, 188–89.
76. Hubmaier, "Freedom, I," 444; Hubmaier, "Schriften," 394.
77. Hubmaier, "Summa," 84–85; Hubmaier, "Schriften," 111.

pledges himself inwardly in his heart to lead a new life after the rule of Christ.[78]

Hubmaier's Understanding of Grace

Another important concept in the consideration of Hubmaier's soteriology is his idea of grace. Grace carries the idea of the undeserved and unmerited divine favor towards humanity. A careful examination of the Anabaptist understanding of grace reveals its divergence from that of Luther and other Magisterial Reformers. The import of the present focus is revealed by the charge that was made in the sixteenth century on the part of the Magisterial Reformers who claimed that the Radical Reformers had no adequate concept of grace.[79]

If Paul is attributed with most discussion related to grace in the New Testament, Augustine is credited for developing the doctrine most powerfully in the history of the Christian church. Augustine's emphasis on the concept of grace was so significant that he became generally known as *doctor gratiae*, "the doctor of grace."[80] The rise in interest in the writings of Paul and Augustine, witnessed in the late Renaissance and Reformation periods, understandably propelled the doctrine of grace to the forefront of Lutheran and Reformed theologies. It is no surprise, therefore, that Luther came to regard the doctrine of grace as the center of the Christian gospel.[81]

The Pauline-Augustinian doctrine of grace held by the Magisterial Reformers "was inseparably linked with the doctrine of divine election, predestination, and the bondage of the will as a consequence of the fall and original sin."[82] It was the forensic view of grace, therefore, "linked with the Pauline anthropology of Rom 6 and 7, and read through Augustinian eyes, that formed the theological standpoint from which the theologians of the Magisterial Reformation accuse the Radicals as having not only an inadequate concept of grace, but also an inadequate concept of sin."[83]

---

78. Beachy, *Grace in the Radical Reformation*, 103; Hubmaier, "Christian Baptism," 115–17; Hubmaier, "Schriften," 134–36.
79. Beachy, *Grace in the Radical Reformation*, 6.
80. McGrath, *Reformation Thought*, 89.
81. Ibid., 188.
82. Beachy, *Grace in the Radical Reformation*, 11.
83. Ibid., 13.

The understanding of grace held by the Magisterial reformers was so extreme in its opposition to man's participation and its fear of adding works to salvation that it led to their theology of faith as a gift from God. This in turn, from the perspective of the Radical Reformers, resulted in stunted sanctification due to the former's misunderstanding of the role of good works. While good works played an important role in Hubmaier's soteriology, they were not determinative for one's salvation. God was ultimately in charge of that. Concomitant with Hubmaier's anthropology, men are responsible for their salvation, yet those who are saved willingly and readily give God all the credit and glory for their redemption. There is for Hubmaier, therefore, both the need of the initial response in salvation on man's part and the utter rejection of ascribing any credit for salvation to that initial response. To misunderstand either part of this statement, as has been done by both the Magisterial Reformers[84] and many subsequent interpreters of Hubmaier's thought,[85] is tantamount to charging the Anabaptist's soteriology with being works-based.

As mentioned above, therefore, Hubmaier's greatest criticism of the aforementioned understanding of grace and works on the part of the theologians of the Magisterial Reformation was that it lacked the desired moral fruits.[86] Hubmaier looked upon the statements made by the Magisterial Reformers, such as, "Faith alone saves us and not our works," and "Our works are worthless before God," as half truths which ultimately make God responsible for all human blasphemies, and which is, therefore, the highest blasphemy of all.[87] Beachy's summary of Hubmaier's concept of grace is quite accurate when he states that for the Radical Reformer, "the claim to the experience of grace is nullified if one does not seize the new possibilities that are opened up for him through the grace of God in Christ."[88] From the Anabaptist perspective, therefore, the failure

---

84. The injustice of this charge has been effectively demonstrated by John C. Wenger, who draws his evidence that the Anabaptists held to absolute dependence of the sinner upon the grace of God for redemption and sanctification from the major Anabaptist writers of all groups—Menno Simons, Dirk Philips, Pilgram Marpeck, and Peter Riedemann, as well as lesser leaders. See Wenger, "Grace and Discipleship in Anabaptism".

85. Jürgen-Goertz fits in this category when he states that "Hubmaier included works in the process of salvation," Jürgen-Goertz, *Anabaptists*, 64.

86. Hubmaier, "Freedom, I," 429; Hubmaier, "Schriften," 381.

87. Hubmaier, "Freedom, I," 429; Hubmaier, "Schriften," 381.

88. Beachy, *Grace in the Radical Reformation*, 31.

to "seize the new possibilities" and the resultant lack of moral earnestness within the Magisterial Reformation, which were noticed by the Radical Reformers and acknowledged by the Magisterials, were the products of the forensic concept of grace.

A twofold concern for the personal and voluntary character of Christian salvation, that compulsion would be a violation of grace on one hand, and for the protection of the moral character of God on the other, causes Hubmaier to make use of the scholastic concepts discussed in the previous chapter, namely a distinction between the absolute will of God and the revealed will of God.[89] The employment of these concepts allows Hubmaier to agree with Luther regarding the fact of predestination, which for the Anabaptist leader was rooted in the sovereignty of God, and yet insist on human responsibility in salvation. According to Hubmaier, confusion in the interpretation of Scriptural texts, such as Rom 9:18, "God has mercy on whom he will; whom he will he hardens," and 1 Tim 2:4, "God wills that all men be saved," is the result of failing to distinguish between two wills.[90] According to God's absolute or secret will, which no one can know since it is hidden from the eye of man, Hubmaier states, "He could consign Peter to hell and conversely raise Judas or Caiphas to heaven and do injustice to no one, since men are in His hands."[91] Making further use of such passages as Mark 16:15; John 1:9, 12; 3:16; and 1 John 2:2; Hubmaier concludes that "according to his preached and revealed will God does not want to harden, darken, or damn anyone except those who want to be hardened, blinded, and damned out of their own evil and freedom of will."[92]

In response to the teaching of the Reformed movement on "irresistible grace," Hubmaier explains that the reference is to God's hidden and not revealed will: "Where one now confuses and mixes the two wills with one another there soon follows out of that a notable misunderstanding, error, and confusion of Scriptures."[93] The Radical Reformer's solution to the present confusion is to "divide the judgments in the Scripture and ruminate truly on them in order to know which Scriptures point to the

---

89. Ibid., 52.
90. Hubmaier, "Freedom of the Will, II," 474; Hubmaier, "Schriften," 418.
91. Hubmaier, "Freedom of the Will, II," 474; Hubmaier, "Schriften," 417.
92. Hubmaier, "Freedom of the Will, II," 472; Hubmaier, "Schriften," 416.
93. Hubmaier, "Freedom of the Will, II," 473; Hubmaier, "Schriften," 417.

secret will of God or to the preached."[94] Even though not all men will be saved, God cannot be held guilty, for He dealt with humanity according to his great mercy and grace:

> The schools call the revealed power and will of God an ordered power and will. Not that the first will is unordered for everything that God wills and does is orderly and good. He is not subject to any rule. His will is itself a rule of all things. Therefore they call the will "ordered" since it occurs according to the preached Word of the Holy Scriptures in which he revealed to us his will. From that now comes the division wherein one speaks of the hidden and the revealed will of God. Not that there are two wills in God, but thus the Scripture serves us and accommodates itself to speak according our human ignorance so that we know that although God is almighty and can do all things omnipotently, nevertheless, he wills not to act toward us poor people according to his omnipotence, but according to his mercy, as he has sufficiently testified the same to us through his most beloved Son and through all those who point to him in the Old and New Testaments.[95]

Aiding the Waldshut preacher's concept of grace was his unique understanding of faith, mentioned briefly in the previous chapter. One of the best definitions of the Radical Reformer's faith is provided in his Catechism:

> Faith is the realization of the unspeakable mercy of God, his gracious favor and goodwill, which he bears to us through his most beloved Son Jesus Christ, whom he did not spare and delivered him to death for our sakes that sin might be paid for, and we might be reconciled to him and with the assurance of our hearts cry to him: Abba, Father, our Father who are in heaven.[96]

Faith is both the work of God, as is made clear in Hubmaier's exegesis of John 6:29 in his *On Christian Baptism*,[97] and man's responsibility, as is evident from his *Freedom of the Will, I*.[98] Hubmaier's grasp of faith as one "that produces the fruits of the Spirit and works through love,"[99] resonates

---

94. Hubmaier, "Freedom of the Will, II," 473; Hubmaier, "Schriften," 417.
95. Hubmaier, "Freedom of the Will, II," 473; Hubmaier, "Schriften," 417.
96. Hubmaier, "Catechism," 348; Hubmaier, "Schriften," 313.
97. Hubmaier, "Christian Baptism," 106; Hubmaier, "Schriften," 127.
98. Hubmaier, "Freedom, I," 440; Hubmaier, "Schriften," 391.
99. Hubmaier, "Catechism," 348; Hubmaier, "Schriften," 313.

well with Bender's description of the general Anabaptist understanding of it as "a dynamic response to God's approach; this response opened the life to the transforming grace of God, which resulted in obedience and discipleship; faith and obedience were as inseparable as regeneration and discipleship. Faith of this sort inevitably produces fruit. Anabaptist faith involved commitment to Christ to follow Him in all things, as Lord, as example, as forerunner."[100]

There may be a parallel, as mentioned before, between the Radical Reformer's multi-faceted concept of faith and that of his medieval predecessors, particularly Gabriel Biel's. Biel held to a double aspect of faith: first, as an act of the intellect initiated by the will, which drives the intellect to a new field of knowledge and thus provides the intellect with a new basis for cognition;[101] and second, as an acquired faith, which is not a product of man's own mind but comes from the outside, a gift from God.[102] It must be emphasized here, with some forcefulness, however, that although some vestiges of Biel's justification may have found their way into Hubmaier's soteriology, the Radical's understanding of salvation certainly does not equate to "justification by works alone" as it apparently did for Biel.[103] Luther, Calvin, and Zwingli obviously rejected that part of Hubmaier's concept of faith that pertained to man's response. Their understanding of faith as a gift lacked the multi-faceted aspect of Hubmaier's faith and also lacked that certain level of responsibility placed by the Anabaptist reformer on man's need to respond to God's work, which was made possible through his trichotomous anthropology.[104]

Faith, for Hubmaier, also played an important role in the relationship between the Word and the Spirit, as argued by Christof Windhorst. According to Windhorst, for Hubmaier, the Word is "consolation and promise, admonition and motivation. As such it is the indispensable presupposition of Spirit baptism and the new birth . . . The preached Word

---

100. Bender, "Walking in the Resurrection," 104.

101. Oberman, *The Harvest of Medieval Theology*, 70; Biel, *Epitome*, III.23.2.I.I.C.

102. Oberman, *The Harvest of Medieval Theology*, 71; Biel, *Epitome*, III.23.2.2.I. In this same section, Biel also mentioned infused faith, although he did not believe it to be a necessity, but helpful to strengthen and perfect the act of faith.

103. Estep, "Anabaptist View," 49.

104. It is the spirit's retention of the pre-fall wholeness that enables man in the first place to respond to the preached word. This concept is reminiscent of the medieval idea of *synderesis*, discussed by Biel and covered earlier in the chapter.

and the Spirit's work follow one another. They are two distinct events and a sinner's understanding does not always come immediately upon hearing the Word."[105] In this context, according to Windhorst's evaluation of Hubmaier's soteriology, the exercise of faith "enables the Spirit of God to make that which is heard come alive so that it begins to live, grow, and bear fruit. As prayer in faith for understanding what is heard is the highest theology, so for Hubmaier, the hearing and believing the Word of God is the greatest honor to God."[106]

THE IMPORT OF CHURCH DISCIPLINE FOR HUBMAIER'S SOTERIOLOGY

With salvation being the final goal of the life-long process of justification and with the import that the church played in that process, as pointed out in the beginning of this chapter, Hubmaier's soteriology resembled more that of the Roman Catholic Church than his Magisterial counterparts. His life-long desire and pursuit to ground his theology in the immovable truths of the Scripture as opposed to the "schoolmen," however, caused Hubmaier to reject the sacramental system of salvation held by the Catholic Church. In place of the sacraments, Hubmaier's soteriology employed the biblical doctrine of church discipline.

In holding that there was no salvation outside of the church, Hubmaier did not share the views of the medieval theologians, namely that only in the church were the sacraments that were necessary for salvation properly administered and received. Instead, the Anabaptist leader associated salvation with the church because of the church's instructional and shepherding role, performed by means of its utilization of the keys, which were, in turn, intimately connected to church discipline. Chapter 4 will focus in detail on the relationship of the keys, implemented through the ordinances, to the doctrine of church discipline.

---

105. "Es ist Tröstung und Verheißung, Ermahnung und Anstoß. Als solches ist es die unerläßliche Voraussetzung von Geisttaufe und Wiedergeburt . . . Predigtwort und Geistwirken folgen aufeinander. Es sind zwei voneinander zu unterscheidende Akte, und nicht immer kommt es zum innerlichen Verstehen des äußerlich gehörten Wortes." See Windhorst, *Täferisches Taufverständnis*, 192.

106. "Nur im Glauben macht der Geist Gottes das Gehörte lebendig, daß es anfängt zu leben, zu grünen und Früchte zu bringen," Windhorst, *Täferisches Taufverständnis*, 192.

Church Discipline and Soteriology 77

For now, however, it will suffice to point out that in baptism the key of loosing was exercised, whereby the portals of the church were open for the forgiving of sins. Baptism, incidentally, was consequential to the Radical's soteriological process due to the intimate bond, mentioned above, between faith and obedience in Hubmaier's understanding of salvation. Baptism was one of the acts of obedience.[107] Hubmaier elaborates on the subject in his Catechism: "For with outward baptism the church opens her doors to all believers who confess their faith orally before her and receives them into her bosom, fellowship, and communion of saints for the forgiveness of their sins. Therefore, as one cares about the forgiveness of his sins and the fellowship of the saints outside of which there is no salvation, just so much should one value water baptism, whereby one enters and is incorporated into the universal Christian church."[108]

Yet, as important as water baptism may have been to the Anabaptist leader's soteriology and for the existence of the local church in his theology, Estep's conclusion is completely accurate when he states that it [baptism] "is never in Hubmaier's thinking a part of the saving process."[109]

The commitment that was made in water baptism by new believers was also *de facto* acquiescence by them to be disciplined by the same church, should the need for it ever arise. In fact, in his *On Fraternal Admonition*, Hubmaier explicitly equates baptism with admonition, the first stage of church discipline.[110] The Radical Reformer again mentions baptism as the first key in his *On the Christian Ban*, stating that after the resurrection Christ gave the church his authority "to baptize . . . in water, thus with the first key opening to her the door the portals of the Christian church, admitting her to the forgiveness of sins."[111]

Likewise, in communion, the key of binding was exercised, by means of which church members were either removed from the communion or, in extreme situations, excommunicated from church membership, as a measure that was supposed to produce repentance and rejection of the sins causing the excommunication in the first place. As with baptism, Hubmaier equates the ban explicitly with communion, stating that "even

---

107. Dyck, "Life of the Spirit in Anabaptism," 316.
108. Hubmaier, "Catechism," 351; Hubmaier, "Schriften," 315.
109. Estep, "Anabaptist View," 45. See also Estep, *Anabaptist Story*, 156–57.
110. Hubmaier, "Admonition," 375; Hubmaier, "Schriften," 339.
111. Hubmaier, "Ban," 412; Hubmaier, "Schriften," 368.

water baptism and the breaking of bread are vain, pointless, and fruitless, if fraternal admonition and the Christian ban do not accompany them, admonition belonging to baptism as the ban belongs to communion and fellowship."[112] Hubmaier elucidates the meaning of the second key further when he writes that with it the church received "the authority to exclude again persons who had been received and admitted into the Christian congregation if they should not will to behave in a right and Christian way, and to close her doors before them."[113]

To recapitulate then, it seems clear that in pursuing biblical foundation for his soteriology, Hubmaier achieved two things. First, he was not willing to absolve men of all responsibility for their salvation as his Magisterial counterparts inadvertently did with their predestenarian grace and forensic justification. Second, unable and unwilling to endorse the sacramental system of the Catholic Church, Hubmaier guarded against lax living, which often characterized the churches and societies of the Magisterial Reformers, with his usage of church discipline as an integral part of the salvation process.

As for the doctrine of sanctification, rather than treating it as a separate subject, Hubmaier included it in his discussion of justification, namely its second stage. In agreement with his Anabaptist contemporaries, Hubmaier saw the "new birth as the transformation of the whole person into the likeness of Christ," thereby avoiding "the Protestant distinction between justification and sanctification."[114] The remainder of this chapter, therefore, will examine the role that church discipline plays in the process of sanctification.

The idea of progressive sanctification is expressed by Hubmaier in terms of the believer receiving, through the living Word, the power to obey the commands of God and to do his will. Through continuous obedience to the will of God, one becomes more and more saintly, or like Christ. This is a human potential.[115] The grace of the second stage of justification operates through the preached Word, which imparts the power that enables the believer to obey God's commands: "Therefore this recognition and power of knowledge, willing, and working must happen

---

112. Hubmaier, "Admonition," 375; Hubmaier, "Schriften," 339.
113. Hubmaier, "Ban," 414; Hubmaier, "Schriften," 370.
114. Ludwig, "Sanctification and Discipline," 81.
115. Mabry, *Doctrine of the Church*, 109.

and be attained by a new grace and drawing of the heavenly Father, who now looks at humanity anew by the merit of Jesus Christ our Lord, blesses and draws him with his life-giving Word which he speaks into the heart of a person . . . Through it God gives power and authority to all people insofar as they themselves want to come; the free choice is left to them."[116]

For Hubmaier, then, aside from what the oft-quoted dictum of Cyprian, "outside the church there is no salvation," has meant for the salvation of the sinner, MacGregor suggests that it also entailed that "one's sanctification could not be sustained apart from the church, for the saints need discipline from their 'mother' in order to maintain holy lives."[117] The reformer asserts, "Where [church discipline] is not instituted and used according to the orderly and earnest command of Christ, there is nothing reigns but sin, scandal and vice."[118] Therefore, in the words of Eddie Mabry, "it was absolutely necessary for Hubmaier . . . that the saint be incorporated into the church."[119] Considering Friedmann's aforementioned claim of the "brotherhood-focused" nature of salvation, the concept of progressive sanctification as an individual process was unthinkable and unknown in the sixteenth-century Anabaptist context.

It is the restored will of the believer, which is not enslaved by sin, that allows Hubmaier to insist upon responsible discipline in the context of the local church. Undergoing the process of church discipline aides the cooperating believer in ridding himself of those sins and entanglements that slow his growth into the likeness of Christ, a process otherwise known as sanctification. Even the uncooperative believer undergoing the ban, or the highest level of discipline, is aided by it, even if unbeknownst to him, in two ways: first, the ban was practiced "not merely to exclude but hopefully to awaken to repentance," and second, when there is no repentance on earth, the ultimate goal of excommunication was the salvation of the spirit, as related in chapter 2, where the Radical Reformer's exposition of 1 Cor 5 was provided.[120]

Although the main test of the authenticity of any given doctrine is its adherence to the Word of God, perhaps a secondary such test may be

---

116. Hubmaier, "Freedom, I," 444; Hubmaier, "Schriften," 394.
117. MacGregor, *European Synthesis*, 33.
118. Hubmaier, "Ban," 410; Hubmaier, "Schriften," 367.
119. Mabry, *Doctrine of the Church*, 73.
120. Hubmaier, "Freedom, I," 434–35; Hubmaier, "Schriften," 386.

in examining the change that it produces in the lives of the believers. If such is the case, Hubmaier's soteriological adherence to the Scriptures has been demonstrated above. As the spokesman of the Anabaptist movement, the ability of Hubmaier's understanding of salvation, as undergirded by the discipline of the church, to produce holy living in his adherents was validated by Prince Philip of Hesse. As someone who had a "keen interest in the religious and moral life of his people," Prince Philip had occasion repeatedly to compare the Anabaptists with Lutherans.[121] On February 18, 1530, in a letter to his neighbor, the Duke of Saxony, in justification of his refusal to accede to the latter's urgent pressure for a policy of harsh persecution of the Anabaptists, Prince Philip expressed the following judgment: "I see more improvement of conduct among those whom we call fanatics [Anabaptists] than among those who are Lutheran."[122] This affirmatory view of Anabaptist sanctification was likewise shared by Zwingli, Bullinger, Schwenckfeld, as well as a mandate of the Council of Bern.[123]

It is the intent of this chapter to identify Hubmaier's doctrine of salvation, including justification and sanctification, in accordance with his own categories. Due to the simple lack of time and necessary conditions to develop his theological thought, Hubmaier, as previously mentioned in chapter 1, was not a systematic theologian. Since Hubmaier's works, as accurately observed by Estep, were "often written in haste, at times in prison, and always to meet an existential need, it is not surprising that there was an unevenness in his works, some errors, and not a few ragged edges."[124]

There is enough information, however, scattered between Hubmaier's treatises, for a "reconstructed" doctrine of salvation, which was precisely the aim of this chapter. In the process of assembling the Radical Reformer's soteriology, his views, as depicted in this chapter, were neither Catholic nor Protestant, if the latter term is descriptive of the Magisterial Reformers' views. Balthasar Hubmaier, by his own admission, was rather a biblicist, where "everything he had ever been taught, every concept, traditional, or reformed, was subjected to a critical analysis in the light of

---

121. Bender, "Walking in the Resurrection," 105.
122. Ibid.
123. Ibid., 106.
124. Estep, "Anabaptist View," 49.

the New Testament. Thus, in agreement with Robert Macoskey's opinion it must be concluded that Hubmaier's beliefs "were first and foremost the results of his New Testament study and the consequent re-thinking of the true nature of the church."[125] Driven by his biblical commitment, therefore, it was the doctrine of church discipline, as clearly demonstrated above, that enabled Hubmaier to keep the proper tension between human responsibility and divine action in his understanding of salvation, without falling into either the works-based justification of the Catholic Church, or, from his perspective, the incomplete understanding of salvation of the Magisterial Reformers.

Having accomplished the goal that was set out in this chapter, it is time now to focus in more detail on the intimate connection in Hubmaier's theology between the doctrine of church discipline and the ordinances as the keys of the kingdom that Jesus Christ left for his church to be exercised until his second coming upon this earth. As such, this will be the focus of the next chapter.

---

125. Macoskey, "Hubmaier's Concept of the Church," 116.

4

Church Discipline and Ecclesiology

INTRODUCTION TO ANABAPTIST ECCLESIOLOGY

Anabaptist theology is "ecclesio-centric," according to the noted twentieth century Mennonite Historian, Cornelius Krahn.[1] This means that if "the Lutheran's central concern is to find God through 'faith alone,' and the Calvinist's chief duty is to do the will of a sovereign God," the chief theological concern of the Anabaptist "centers around the *ecclesia*."[2] Robert Friedmann's comments contrasting the individualistic nature of the present Protestant understanding of salvation to the "brotherhood-minded" Anabaptist concept of the same, while quoted in the previous chapter, are also instructive and befitting the current emphasis on the church:

> Now then, the central idea of Anabaptism, the real dynamite in the age of Reformation, as I see it, was this, that one cannot find salvation without caring for his brother, that this "brother" actually matters in the personal life . . . This interdependence of men gives life and salvation a new meaning. It is not "faith alone" which matters (for which faith no church organization would be needed)

---

1. Krahn, "Prolegomena," 11.

2. Ibid., 10. Menno Simons, for example, is reported to have said, while on his sickbed—which was to become his deathbed—that nothing on earth was as precious to him as the church, Zijpp, "The Conception of Our Fathers Regarding the Church," 91.

but it is brotherhood, this intimate caring for each other, as it was commanded to the disciples of Christ as the way to God's kingdom. That was the discovery which made Anabaptism so forceful and outstanding in all of church history.[3]

If this is so, then Krahn's directive to keep this "ecclesio-centric" approach in mind in order to understand and evaluate properly early Anabaptist theology should be carefully heeded.[4] Consequently, any consideration of the doctrinal edifice of Balthasar Hubmaier must include an examination of his doctrine of the church. This chapter will focus particularly on Hubmaier's understanding of the ordinances of baptism and the Lord's Supper and their intimate connection to church discipline.

Hubmaier's doctrine of the church was typical of the Anabaptist understanding in the sixteenth century. The only area where he departed from the mainstream Anabaptist ecclesiology was in his teaching on the sword.[5] A full appreciation of Hubmaier's ecclesiology and his understanding of the ordinances in particular requires some familiarity with the immediate context of the Radical's thought, especially as it contrasted to both the Catholic and the Classical Reformers' doctrines of the church. In the process of the unfolding examination, therefore, an effort will be made to provide such contextual information as much as possible.

From the Roman Catholic perspective, the church was a visible, historic institution possessing historical continuity with the apostolic church.[6] The Magisterial Reformers, convinced that the Catholic Church had lost sight of the doctrine of justification by faith alone, as *the articulus stantis et cadentis ecclesiae*, "the article by which the church stands or falls," concluded that it had lost its claim to be considered as the authentic Christian church.[7] Both Luther and the Reformed theologians viewed the church as the mixed body of the just and the unjust, leaving the job of sorting between the two to the Lord alone. Consequently, the Magisterial

---

3. Friedmann, "On Mennonite Historiography," 121.

4. Krahn, "Prolegomena," 11.

5. His teaching on the sword, where he regarded the coercive powers of government as something of a necessary evil and held that Christians could hold office as magistrates without compromising their integrity, was not typical of Anabaptism as a whole. See Hubmaier, "Sword"; Hubmaier, "Schriften". The part of ecclesiology which is concerned with the church's social interaction, however, lies outside of the scope of this research.

6. McGrath, *Reformation Thought*, 188.

7. Ibid.

Reformers were unwilling to go as far as agreeing with the Radicals that the possibility existed of establishing the true church on earth, the one consisting of only the regenerated believers and no institution of other kind merited the name church of God. In their attempt to claim the middle ground between the Catholic and the Radical views, the theologians of the Magisterial Reformation found themselves involved in serious inconsistencies.[8] So much so that Alister E. McGrath describes their views on the church as the "Achilles' heel" of the Magisterial Reformers.[9]

The Radical Reformation conceived of the church as being in but not of the world. Persecuted by the Catholic Church on one side and the Magisterial Reformers on the other, the theologians of the Anabaptist persuasion spoke of the church "as an 'alternative society' within the mainstream of sixteenth-century European culture. Just as the pre-Constantinian church existed within the Roman Empire, yet refused to conform to its standards, so the radical Reformation envisaged itself existing parallel to, but not within, its sixteenth-century environment . . . This notion of the church as a faithful remnant in conflict with the world harmonized with the Anabaptist experience of persecution by the forces of Antichrist, personified in the magistracy."[10]

The great church historian, Philip Schaff relates well the difference between the types of churches envisioned by the Magisterial and Radical Reformers: "The [Magisterial] reformers aimed to reform the old Church by the Bible; the radicals attempted to build a new Church from the Bible."[11] The Radicals, to be more precise, attempted to restore the biblical idea of the church as prescribed in the New Testament. In other words, in contrast to the apostolic succession of the Catholic Church, the Anabaptists understood "apostolicity" to mean "true to the apostolic church."[12] Later Schaff goes on to add that the "Reformers found

---

8. One of the inconsistencies in which the Magisterial Reformers were caught was that of accepting Augustine's view of the church, inspired by the parable of the tares in Matt 13:24–31, as a "mixed" body, as opposed to the Radicals' more Donatist view of the church as a body of the just, and the just alone, and yet breaking away from the Catholic Church. For if the church is a mixed body, it implies that there will always be corruption in the true church.

9. McGrath, *Reformation Thought*, 188.

10. Ibid., 202.

11. Schaff, *History of the Reformation: 1517–1648*, 71.

12. Littell, "The Anabaptist Church," 126.

a popular state-church, including all the citizens with their families; the Anabaptists organized on the voluntary principle select congregations of baptized believers, separated from the world and from the State."[13] Thomas M. Lindsay clarifies the difference between the Magisterial and Radical Reformers further:

> The Anabaptists would have nothing to do with a state Church; and this was the main point in their separation from the Lutherans, Zwinglians, and Calvinists. It was perhaps the *one* conception on which all parties among them were in absolute accord. The real Church, which might be small or great, was for them an association of believing people; and the great ecclesiastical institutions into which unconscious infants were admitted by a ceremony called baptism long before they could have or exercise faith, represented to them an idea subversive of true Christianity.[14]

According to Franklin H. Littell, in the interpretation of history common to the theologians of the Radical Reformation, the early church was the heroic age and its life and style were normative for true believers.[15] The epoch following the early church period witnessed a fall of the church, according to the Anabaptist understanding.[16] Alvin J. Beachy expresses well this Anabaptist notion stating that there was "an almost universal conviction among the Radicals that either at some particular *point in history,* or during a period of time sufficiently far removed from the apostolic age to allow abuses to creep into the Church's life, she had fallen . . . from her apostolic foundation."[17] This fallen state of the church, according to the Anabaptist view, was precipitated by Constantine's recognition of the church and its alignment with the state and it lasted from the days of Constantine until the beginning of their own movement.[18] This union of church and state, in fact, became one of the marks of a

---

13. Schaff, *History of the Reformation: 1517–1648*, 71.

14. Lindsay, *The Reformation in Switzerland, France, the Netherlands, Scotland and England*, 443.

15. Littell, "The Anabaptist Church," 127.

16. For an excellent discussion of the various issues regarding the fall of the church, see Littell, *The Anabaptist View of the Church*, 46–78; and for an excellent overview of the dates when the fall of the church supposedly occurred, which is based upon primary sources, see Garrett, "Nature of the Church," 112–13.

17. Beachy, *Grace in the Radical Reformation*, 87 (emphasis present).

18. Littell, *The Anabaptist View of the Church*, 64. The Classical Reformers, incidentally, also belonged to the period of the Fall according to the Anabaptists.

fallen church in the Anabaptist understanding.[19] The centuries following the fall, according to Littell, were the time during which "imperial arrogance, hierarchical ambition, and baptized heathenism were blended together in politico-religious union."[20]

In contrast to the Classical Reformation's desire to reform the church, the Radicals believed that it had to be restituted. Frank J. Wray, in his article "The Anabaptist Doctrine of the Restitution of the Church," defines correctly this chasm between the Magisterial and the Radical ideas of mending the church:

> The key concept of the Reformers was *reformatio*. From their point of view the remnant remained within the Great Church. The task at hand was to free the Great Church from the control of the papal Antichrist and to remove the abominations which had been introduced. The fundamental concept among the Anabaptists was *restitutio*. The medieval church was beyond hope. The children of God must be recalled from exile. They must rebuild the true church upon apostolic foundations. They must separate themselves from the fallen church, which was now the church of Antichrist.[21]

The task of the Radical Reformation, therefore, as seen by their own theologians, was to restitute the true church and "this radical program included vastly more than the elimination of the most heathenish cults which had accumulated or the abandonment of false or unnecessary teachings."[22] The church, according to Anabaptists, needed to be restituted because it was so corrupt that it could not be reformed, so the only thing that could be done was "to go back to the period before the initial fall of the church, and to restore the church to the purity of the New Testament and the Golden Age of Faith."[23] This restored true church, in Littell's

---

19. According to Littell, the other marks of the fallen church were: (2) the widespread of war, (3) the rise of the hierarchy within the church, (4) the power and wealth of the papacy, (5) infant baptism, by which countless numbers of unregenerated people had been brought into the church, and (6) the church's involvement in the persecution of heretics, attempting to force people to have faith or to believe the right things. See Littell, *The Anabaptist View of the Church*, 64–72.

20. Littell, "The Anabaptist Church," 127.

21. Wray, "The Anabaptist Doctrine of the Restitution of the Church," 186.

22. Littell, "The Anabaptist Church," 127.

23. Mabry, *Doctrine of the Church*, 90.

words, "was to recapitulate apostolic life and virtue."[24] Furthermore, since the fall of the church had been brought about by union with the state, the restored church was to be separated from the state.[25]

HUBMAIER'S ECCLESIOLOGY

As mentioned previously in this work, although there are numerous similarities between Anabaptist ecclesiology and Balthasar Hubmaier's doctrine of the church, a considerable list of dissimilarities points to Hubmaier as a theologian in his own right, who, while influenced by the Anabaptist ecclesiology, made a deliberate choice to ground his theology in the Word of God, rather than simply adhering to any particular movement of the day. Considering the general circumstances that called forth Hubmaier's writings, the subject of the church receives by far the largest amount of attention.[26] Central to the practically-focused theology of the Anabaptist leader, the doctrine of the church, in the words of Eddie Mabry, "was gradually and painfully forged out of persecution and turmoil."[27]

Whereas a systematic study of Hubmaier's ecclesiology as a whole may require some "assembly,"[28] as he was "far too busy addressing the pressing issues of the day, to spend time writing a systematic presentation of his doctrine of the church,"[29] a particular study of his theology of ordinances needs nothing of the sort. For the Radical Reformer's theology of baptism and the Lord's Supper is divided, for the most part, between the following works: *Summa of the Entire Christian Life, On the Christian Baptism of Believers, Old and New Teachers on Believers Baptism, Dialogue with Oecolampad on Infant Baptism, Dialogue with Zwingli's Baptism*

---

24. Littell, "The Anabaptist Church," 127.
25. Mabry, *Doctrine of the Church*, 90.
26. Vedder, *Hübmaier*, 201.
27. Mabry, *Doctrine of the Church*, 69.
28. The following three treatises alone contain sufficient information regarding Hubmaier's ecclesiology: Hubmaier, "Twelve Articles in Prayer"; Hubmaier, "Schriften"; Hubmaier, "Apologia"; Hubmaier, "Schriften"; Hubmaier, "Catechism"; Hubmaier, "Schriften".
29. Mabry, *Doctrine of the Church*, 69.

Book, *The Ground and Reason, A Form for Water Baptism, Several Theses Concerning the Mass,* and *A Form for Christ's Supper.*

In his Catechism, Hubmaier identifies the church in the clearest and perhaps most comprehensive way of any one particular statement in his writings:

> The church is sometimes understood to include all the people who are gathered and united in one God, one Lord, one faith, and one baptism, and have confessed this faith with their mouths, wherever they may be on earth. This, then, is the universal Christian corporeal church and fellowship of the saints, assembled only in the Spirit of God, as we confess in the ninth article of our creed. At other times the church is understood to mean each separate and outward meeting assembly or parish membership that is under one shepherd or bishop and assembles bodily for instruction, for baptism and the Lord's Supper. The church as daughter has the same power to bind and to loose on earth as the universal church, her mother, when she uses the keys according to the command of Christ, her spouse and husband.[30]

This text, along with all other references to the church in Hubmaier's works, represents well the importance the doctrine of church discipline plays in the reformer's ecclesiology. If, as this work has endeavored to demonstrate thus far, the doctrine of church discipline was important in the cases of the reformer's anthropology and soteriology, it was absolutely crucial in the present case of his ecclesiology. So much so, that without church discipline, there would be no doctrine of the church for Balthasar Hubmaier. The truth of this statement can be seen in his understanding of the exercise of the keys as the primary responsibility and obligation of the church on earth. The keys, which in Hubmaier's mind, were intimately connected to the ordinances, which in turn, were joined with various stages of church discipline, illustrate the significance that the latter played in his ecclesiology. The rest of this chapter will substantiate and elaborate on the current claim.

As is evident from the Waldshut preacher's Catechism statement quoted above, Hubmaier understood the church to exist both universally and locally as visible bodies, unified by a common faith and built upon a public profession of this faith.[31] The local church was the daughter

---

30. Hubmaier, "Catechism," 351–52; Hubmaier, "Schriften," 315.
31. Mabry, *Doctrine of the Church*, 70.

Church Discipline and Ecclesiology

of the universal church, and shared equally in the latter's shepherding responsibilities and the powers of the keys.[32]

Witness was one of the key functions of the church in Hubmaier's mind. According to Robert A. Macoskey, Hubmaier sees "the Great Commission as binding on every member of the fellowship and interprets Christ's command literally."[33] Believing that witness was a fundamental part of the church, Hubmaier emerges as one of the earliest advocates of the modern missionary movement.[34] The reformer understood that every believer received an internal quickening at the moment of conversion and was under the obligation to evangelize. In Hubmaier's view, no vast educational background was necessary for the believer to share his faith.[35] According to Macoskey's overview of Hubmaier's concept of witness, the reformer believed that "faith and hope were his [believer's] credentials; the gospel was his warrant. He found encouragement and direction for his labor in the fellowship of other believers."[36]

Hubmaier's typically Anabaptist concept of church included only those who were regenerated saints. For the Radical Reformer, the word "saint" meant those believers who were regenerated and lived their lives according to the rules of Christ as set forth in the New Testament.[37] There were certain prerequisites set out by Hubmaier for becoming a saint and for being included in the church.[38] First, one had to undergo a baptism in the Spirit, a genuine inner regenerating experience which preceded water baptism.[39] This will be discussed in greater detail in the section discussing baptism. Hubmaier's second prerequisite for saints was to see their inner regeneration followed by water baptism, which was a witness or a sign of the former.[40] The Anabaptist leader makes this point quite clearly and

---

32. Ibid.

33. Macoskey, "Hubmaier's Concept of the Church," 112.

34. Ibid.

35. Ibid.

36. Ibid.

37. Mabry, *Doctrine of the Church*, 71.

38. Eddie Mabry first pointed out these prerequisites in an organized way in his Mabry, *Doctrine of the Church*, 70–73. The following list of prerequisites therefore, is assembled in consultation with his manuscript.

39. Hubmaier, "Christian Baptism," 100–102, 145; Hubmaier, "Schriften," 122–23, 159.

40. Mabry, *Doctrine of the Church*, 71.

forcefully in his *On the Christian Ban*: "He then who confesses Christian faith, accepts the sign of water baptism according to the institution of Christ, and argues no more."[41] The third prerequisite for the saint, according to Hubmaier, was conscientious and willing affiliation with the local church accomplished through believer's baptism. While excluding infant baptism, this particular prerequisite also underlined the import that church membership, of which baptism was an initiation, played in one's salvation and sanctification. Finally, the living of saintly lives according to the clear teaching of Scripture was an important fourth prerequisite for the saint in Hubmaier's theology:

> One should ask the Scriptures and not the church, for God wants to have from us only his law and his will, not our stubborn heads or opinions. God is more interested in obedience to his words than in all our sacrifices and even the self-devised church practices, as we have it in all the divine writings of the prophets, the twelve apostles, and the saints. The greatest and right honor that we can offer to God is to keep his Word and live according to his will, not according to our laws and opinions.[42]

This last was, according to Mabry, a "prime prerequisite" for Hubmaier's saints.[43] The living of godly lives, in the reformer's doctrine of the church was what distinguished the Anabaptist churches from the corruption and immorality of the Catholics and Magisterial Reformers.[44]

ORDINANCES AS KEYS OF THE KINGDOM

An informed discussion of Hubmaier's theology of the ordinances must commence with his doctrine of the keys. The reason this is so is because, according to Carl M. Leith's accurate analysis of the Radical's theology, Hubmaier himself "insists that the proper understanding of the keys is foundational to the proper understanding and practice of the sacraments."[45] Hubmaier's understanding of the powers of the church was expressed through its exercise of the keys. Belonging originally to God,

---

41. Hubmaier, "Ban," 420; Hubmaier, "Schriften," 374.
42. Hubmaier, "Dialogue," 181; Hubmaier, "Schriften," 176.
43. Mabry, *Doctrine of the Church*, 74.
44. Ibid.
45. Leth, "Hubmaier's Catholic Exegesis," 114.

Church Discipline and Ecclesiology

this power was transferred to Christ at his incarnation and to the church at the time of Jesus' ascension: "as his Heavenly Father has given the same to him, in heaven and on earth, and as Christ used the same in teaching and in deed, as he walked among us bodily. But when he was to ascend into heaven and to sit at the right hand of his almighty Father, no longer remaining bodily with us on earth, just then he hung this power and these keys at the side of his most beloved spouse and bride."[46]

Mabry's able explanation provides a pertinent visual image of Hubmaier's understanding of the way in which Jesus transferred the power of the keys to his church: "Christ, having received the power of the keys from God, before He ascended into heaven, 'girded' his spouse with the power. The image was of Christ literally preparing the church for warfare, as one who girds the sword on another to do battle. The power of the keys would be that by which the church would protect and maintain herself; thus Christ 'girded' her with the power of the keys."[47]

This power of the keys, according to Hubmaier, was given to the church as a whole and not to its leadership, or any one person:

> He [Christ] said to Peter . . . "I will give to you the keys of the kingdom of Heaven" . . . When Christ says, "To you," he signifies the unity of the church . . . The church never had this power before the resurrection of Christ, for although John and the disciples of Christ preached and baptized with water before the resurrection of Christ, they never pointed those who were baptized to the church for the forgiveness of their sins. For at that time the church had received no keys from Christ, but rather they pointed, drove, and brought to Christ the newly born and baptized disciples (whom they had led to an awareness of their sins). He himself received them, forgave them their sins, opened up to them the gates of Christian fellowship, and took them into his holy communion.[48]

Of the two keys given to the church, the first was the key of forgiveness, or loosing, by which the church exercised the power it received from Christ to open the doors of heaven to that sinner who was truly repentant of sin and to receive that sinner into the community of saints.[49] This key was very important for Hubmaier and the Anabaptists, for it insured,

---

46. Hubmaier, "Ban," 411; Hubmaier, "Schriften," 368.
47. Mabry, *Doctrine of the Church*, 77.
48. Hubmaier, "Ban," 411–12; Hubmaier, "Schriften," 368–69.
49. Mabry, *Doctrine of the Church*, 78.

in their understanding, that their congregations were truly regenerated. Franklin H. Littell points to this very aspect of the first key stating that in the view of the Anabaptists "if the door of entrance were closely watched, a strong and true church could be maintained."[50]

There were two exercises of the key of loosing or forgiveness: the initial forgiveness of sins of those who were to be incorporated into the church, given at baptism, and the forgiveness of sins of those previously under the ban.[51] The church, in Hubmaier's theology, actually had the power to forgive or not to forgive one's sins: "It follows that the Christian church now has this authority to forgive and to retain sins here on earth."[52]

The second key which Christ gave to his church, according to Hubmaier, was the key of binding or brotherly admonition, exercised through the Communion. By means of this key the straying believers were separated from the fellowship of the Supper, and, in worst case scenario excommunicated from the membership of the church.[53] According to the University of Northern Iowa historian, Kirk R. McGregor, Hubmaier's understanding of the keys was unique, in that it was focused on the doors which they unlocked, into and out of the kingdom of heaven: "Following his scholastic forebears Peter Lombard, Bonaventure, and Aquinas, the radical fixed the number of keys at two; but unlike these medieval thinkers, who regarded the keys as the divinely bestowed priestly powers to determine appropriate penance for and subsequently remit sin, Hubmaier shifted the disciplinary function from the keys to their two respective doors, one leading into and the other leading out of the kingdom of heaven."[54]

Water baptism, therefore, serves as the key of loosing and the Communion constitutes the key of binding: "For in water baptism the church uses the key of admitting and loosing, but in the Supper the key of excluding, binding, and locking away."[55]

What is of particular interest regarding the reformer's understanding of church discipline in the context of his ecclesiology, therefore, is not

---

50. Littell, *The Anabaptist View of the Church*, 85.
51. Mabry, *Doctrine of the Church*, 81.
52. Hubmaier, "Ban," 414; Hubmaier, "Schriften," 370.
53. Hubmaier, "Ban," 414; Hubmaier, "Schriften," 370.
54. MacGregor, *European Synthesis*, 159.
55 . Hubmaier, "Dialogue," 175; Hubmaier, "Schriften," 171.

Church Discipline and Ecclesiology 93

only its connection to the two ordinances, namely, baptism and the Lord's Supper, but especially its association of the ordinances with the keys. The reason that Hubmaier's doctrine of church discipline is so closely connected to the ordinances is because the ordinances, in his mind, encapsulated the whole gamut of biblical theology: "The water concerns God, the Supper our neighbors; therein lie all the Law and the Prophets."[56] Later in the same treatise Hubmaier re-affirms this idea when he states that by loving "the Lord my God . . . and my neighbor as myself . . . I have fulfilled the Law and the Prophets."[57] Thus, the ordinances of baptism and the Lord's Supper, integral for the proper administration of church discipline, illustrate that which, in Hubmaier's view is the "sum of all preaching."[58]

In summary, the power of loosing and binding was given by Christ to the church to be used through its exercise of church discipline in the context of the ordinances. In empowering the church to do so, Christ swore that he would uphold it in its disciplinary decisions. What was included in the church and by the church on earth, therefore, would be included in heaven; and what was excluded from the church would likewise be excluded in heaven.[59] In the church age, while Christ is absent from this world, the keys of the kingdom belong to the universal church, which alone has the authority to bind and loose people, whose judgments stand in eternity, and which exercises this unique power through its practice of the ordinances.[60]

As this work turns to the consideration of the ordinances of water baptism and the Lord's Supper and their interrelation with the doctrine of church discipline, John Rempel's comprehension of the reformer's doctrine of ordinances in the light of his anthropology serves as a good introduction: "From the vantage point of his older anthropology, Hubmaier was convinced that belief in both the bondage of the will and predestination violates the biblical picture of the human will and undermines human responsibility before God. On this foundation, Hubmaier makes his

---

56. Hubmaier, "Catechism," 355; Hubmaier, "Schriften," 318.
57. Hubmaier, "Catechism," 359; Hubmaier, "Schriften," 321.
58. Hubmaier, "Catechism," 359; Hubmaier, "Schriften," 321.
59. Mabry, *Doctrine of the Church*, 82.
60. Hubmaier, "Ban," 411; Hubmaier, "Schriften," 368.

most radical assertion: baptism and the Lord's Supper are human acts of commitment in response to grace."[61]

BAPTISM

On Easter Day, April 16, 1525, and the three days following, Balthasar Hubmaier baptized three hundred adults of Waldshut using water from a milk pail.[62] He had been baptized himself along with sixty others by Wilhelm Reublin just the day before.[63] As important as baptism was to the overall theology of the Radical Reformer, it is no coincidence that a baptismal ceremony was used to introduce Anabaptist reform into the little town of Waldshut.

Hubmaier, according to William R. Estep, was "the most able sixteenth-century defender of the Anabaptist position on baptism."[64] Harvard historian George Huntston Williams fine-tunes Estep's assertion by enumerating some seven or eight variant baptismal theologies, implicit or explicit, in the Radical Reformation and identifying Hubmaier's as "the baptismal theology of two covenants."[65] Williams' assertion, however, is only partially accurate. With his "distinction in the historical roles of the law and the Gospel, and the related distinction between John and Jesus," according to Rollin S. Armour's admission, "Hubmaier had all the material necessary for interpreting redemptive history in terms of the two covenants, as later Anabaptism did so effectively."[66] Yet, in Armour's correct analysis, the reformer "did not move in the direction of two covenants . . .

---

61. Rempel, *The Supper*, 45.

62. Armour, *Anabaptist Baptism*, 19.

63. Ibid.

64. Estep, *Anabaptist Story*, 149.

65. Williams, *The Radical Reformation*, 440. Among others in Williams's list were (1) the baptismal theology of three degrees or intensities (Denck, Hut, Schiemer, Hutter); (2) the covenantal-bethrothal concept (Campanus, Hofmann); (3) the Melchiorite-Münsterite baptism as the eschatological civic pledge; (4) the deificatory theory of believers' baptism (Servetus); (5) the immersionist imitation of Christ as prophet, priest, and king among the Polish Brethren; (6) the humane-magical defense of baptism for infants and the insane (Paracelsus); and (7) the interiorization of spiritualization of baptism to the point where it is replaced by an all-embracing eucharistic theology or predestinarian regeneration or ethical transformation (Schwenckfeld, Ascherham, Denck, Bünderlin, Entfelder in their final phase; Camillo Renato, Jacob Palaeologus, Faustus Socinus).

66. Armour, *Anabaptist Baptism*, 39.

but preferred to speak of a single covenant available to the Old Testament faithful in promise and to believers in reality."[67] Baptism was particularly significant subject for the Radical Reformer, as is evident not only from the opening statement, but also from the fact that six of the eleven books and treatises which he devoted to the ordinances pertained to it.

To say that Hubmaier rejected the sacramental view of the baptism and the Lord's Supper of his mother church[68] would be accurate on one hand and a gross oversimplification on the other. The Radical Reformer did, in fact, reject the Catholic understanding of baptism as the remedy for original sin.[69] Hubmaier further denied that baptism and the Lord's Supper were sacraments conferring grace *ex opere operato*, on the basis of the performance of the rites. Yet, rather than stopping there, Hubmaier reinterpreted the concept of sacrament, moving it away from the elements of water, bread and wine to the human commitment that was made in partaking of the elements: "We have called the water of baptism, like the bread and the wine of the altar, a 'sacrament'; and held it to be such, although not the water, bread, or wine, but in the fact that the baptismal commitment or the pledge of love is really and truly 'sacrament' in the Latin; i.e., a commitment by oath and a pledge given by the hand which the one baptized makes to Christ."[70]

Hubmaier always maintained that both ordinances were extremely important to one's growth in sanctification. While the significance and particular meaning assigned to each ordinance will be described below, Kirk MacGregor's summation of Hubmaier's understanding of baptism serves as a good introduction into the discussion of the present subject: "just as human freedom is the *sine qua non* of theology, so believers' baptism is the *sine qua non* of the church."[71] Hubmaier himself expresses this thought clearly in his *On the Christian Baptism of Believers*: "Where there is no water baptism, there is no church nor

---

67. Ibid.

68. At the time of the Reformation the Roman Catholic Church taught that baptism was essential to salvation, that it was efficacious for the washing away of original sin and all sins committed up to baptism, that it conveyed divine grace automatically (*ex opere operato*), and that it should be administered to infants at the earliest possible moment, since they are lost without baptism, Harold S. Bender, "Baptism," 224.

69. Steinmetz, *Reformers in the Wings*, 142.

70. Hubmaier, "A Form for Water Baptism," 391; Hubmaier, "Schriften," 352.

71. MacGregor, *European Synthesis*, 152.

minister, neither brother nor sister, no brotherly admonition, excommunication, or reacceptance. I am speaking here of the visible church as Christ did in Matt 18:15ff. There must also exist an outward confession or testimony through which visible brothers and sisters can know each other, since faith exists only in the heart."[72]

In agreeing with Luther that the church is built not on Peter but on his confession of faith, Hubmaier indicates that believers make this same declaration of faith through baptism.[73] Consequently, faith had to precede baptism in Hubmaier's theology. He writes of it in his *On the Christian Baptism of Believers*: "in order to manifest to other believers in Christ his heart, mind, faith, and intention, he joins their brotherhood and churches, so that from now on he might interact with them and they again with him as with a Christian. Therefore, he accepts and gives a public testimony of his internal faith and lets himself be baptized with water."[74]

Pointing to both the way that words were arranged in Scripture and the sequence of preaching, believing, baptizing in the Great Commission, Hubmaier insisted in all of his writings that the true baptism was the baptism of those who believe.[75] Commenting on the relation between Spirit baptism and baptism by water in Hubmaier's theology, Hans Jürgen-Goertz asserted, "As the inner preceded the outer, faith had to come before water-baptism."[76] As such, since faith was a prerequisite for baptism and Hubmaier's concept of faith, unlike that of the Magisterial Reformers, was not simply that of a divine gift, the Radical chose not practice or endorse infant baptism.[77] For baptism which is not preceded by faith was invalid for Hubmaier. The reason for this was Hubmaier's ardent conviction that water baptism itself does not save one, belief does. He articulates this clearly in his *Dialogue with Zwingli's Baptism Book*:

> We know well that salvation is bound neither to baptism nor to works of mercy. Being unbaptized does not condemn us, nor do evil works, but only unfaith. However, whoever is believing lets himself be baptized and bring forth good fruits. Accordingly, if

72. Hubmaier, "Christian Baptism," 127; Hubmaier, "Schriften," 145.
73. Hubmaier, "Catechism," 351–54; Hubmaier, "Schriften," 315–17.
74. Hubmaier, "Christian Baptism," 117; Hubmaier, "Schriften," 136.
75. Mabry, *Doctrine of the Church*, 132.
76. Jürgen-Goertz, *Anabaptists*, 74.
77. For more comprehensive discussion of Hubmaier's sentiments with regard to infant baptism, see Armour, *Anabaptist Baptism*, 21–30.

one wants to be a Christian and if he has a baptizer and water at hand, then he lets himself be baptized by virtue of the institution of Christ. If he does not do it, however, then he is not condemned because of his non-baptism, but because of his unfaith, from which his disobedience proceeds.[78]

Hubmaier communicates the same sentiment in his *A Form for Christ's Supper*: "We do not believe because we have been baptized in water, but we are baptized in water because we first believe."[79] Hubmaier discerned three separate types of baptism in the Scripture: the Spirit baptism, water baptism, and baptism by blood.[80] While it is water baptism that is of particular consequence for the purpose of this chapter, a brief mention of the baptism of the Spirit and of the blood will be made here first for the sake of clarity.

Baptism of the Spirit

Baptism of the Spirit was first for Hubmaier not only in the order of sequence but also of importance.[81] Hubmaier's doctrine of the Spirit baptism, according to Mabry's summation, is "the Spirit of God working through the Word of God in the heart of the sinner to lead to a confession of sins, and to a restoration of wholeness."[82] This "restoration of wholeness," in Hubmaier's understanding was a process involving several

78. Hubmaier, "Dialogue," 191; Hubmaier, "Schriften," 183.

79. Hubmaier, "A Form for Supper," 398; Hubmaier, "Schriften," 358.

80. In response to Zwingli's assertion that there are four baptisms, Hubmaier identified five kinds of baptism in his *On the Christian Baptism of Believers*: (1) outward water baptism, that is, simple form with no limiting content as such; (2) water baptism unto change of life, that is, baptism which contains commitment to live by the Rule of Christ; (3) baptism in the Spirit and fire, that is, baptism emphasizing the work of the Spirit of God inwardly; (4) rebirth out of water and the Spirit, likewise an inward baptism; (5) baptism in the name of the Trinity or in the name of Christ—one of confession and commitment leading to missions involvement and eventually to persecution, Hubmaier, "Christian Baptism," 99; Hubmaier, "Schriften," 121. He fine-tunes this list in his *Dialogue with Zwingli's Baptism Book* condensing the previous five categories to the three categories, which will be discussed in this work, Hubmaier, "Dialogue," 189; Hubmaier, "Schriften," 182. For more detailed discussion of the progression of Hubmaier's baptismal theology within his treatises, see Pipkin, "The Baptismal Theology" and Windhorst, *Täferisches Taufverständnis*, 21–146.

81. For an excellent discussion of Hubmaier's doctrine of the baptism of the Spirit, see Windhorst, *Täferisches Taufverständnis*, 183–213.

82. Mabry, *Doctrine of the Church*, 134.

steps. First step was the hearing of the preached Word of God as the only way by which one can hear, believe, and trust God.[83] The second step was the recognition of sins resulting from the preached Word of God.[84] Third step was turning to God as a signal of giving up on becoming able to do anything about sin.[85] Finally, the fourth step was the final surrender of the sinner to Christ.[86] Hubmaier identifies the baptism of the Spirit in his *On the Christian Baptism of Believers* as: "Baptism in the Spirit and fire is to make alive and whole again the confessing sinner with the fire of the divine Word by the Spirit of God. This takes place when the pardon of his sins has already been granted him by the life-giving Word of God. The Spirit of God makes and effects this enlivening internally in the human being. Outside of the same all teaching of the Word is a killing letter."[87]

Baptism of the Blood

In light of the intense persecution experienced by the Anabaptists for their distinctive theology of water baptism for believers only, it is no surprise to find that baptism of the blood, according to Hubmaier, came as a necessary consequence of the baptism of the Spirit and of the water.[88] The Radical Reformer's concept of the baptism of the blood included both suffering or dying for the faith, as well as the daily killing of the old Adam in human beings.[89] Hubmaier explains in his *A Brief Apologia* how one should enter it joyfully knowing that one could not expect to identify with Christ in glory without first identifying with Him in suffering, through the baptism of blood:

> For I confess three kinds of baptism: that of the Spirit, which takes place inwardly in faith; the second, of water, which takes place outwardly by oral affirmation of faith before the church; and the third of blood in martyrdom or on the deathbed, of which Christ

83. Ibid., 135.
84. Ibid.
85. Ibid., 136.
86. Ibid.
87. Hubmaier, "Christian Baptism," 100; Hubmaier, "Schriften," 121.
88. For more detailed discussion of the baptism of the blood, see Armour, *Anabaptist Baptism*, 42.
89. Windhorst defines the baptism of the blood as the "daily killing of the flesh until the end of life" (die tägliche Tötung des Fleisches bis an das Ende des Lebens), Windhorst, *Täferisches Taufverständnis*, 177.

also speaks . . . John calls these three baptisms, with which all Christians must be baptized, the three witnesses on earth, 1 John 5:7. For whoever wants to cry with Christ to God: "Abba, pater, dear Father," must do so in faith, and must also be cobaptized in water with Christ and suffer jointly with him in blood. Then he will be a son and heir of God, fellow heir with Christ, and will be jointly glorified with Christ, Rom 8:17. Therefore no one should be terrified of persecution or suffering, for Christ had to suffer and thus enter into his glory, Luke 24:26. And also Paul writes: "All who desire to live so devoutly in Christ Jesus will be persecuted," 2 Tim 3:12.[90]

Water Baptism

Hubmaier's baptismal theology subsumed the following progression: the Word of God compels the listener to repent, inner baptism "purifies the heart of its evil conscience" and only then comes "outward baptism," which, "without the internal baptism . . . is only hypocrisy."[91] When it came to water baptism, therefore, Hubmaier believed that it presupposed the inner baptism of the Spirit, which validated the former.[92] Hence, in Hubmaier's theology, unlike the traditional medieval theology or the theologies of the Magisterial Reformers, the outer baptism by water did not bring about the inner baptism of the Spirit.[93]

According to Hubmaier, the desire to partake of water baptism was present within all who were baptized by the Spirit. He further believed that water baptism was a public, outer, and visible expression of obedience to the Lord by those who had experienced a private, inner, and invisible

---

90. Hubmaier, "A Brief Apologia," 301; Hubmaier, "Schriften," 275.

91. Hubmaier, "Old & New Teachers," 262; Hubmaier, "Schriften," 239.

92. Baptism of John which lies outside of the limited scope of this work must be mentioned here as a theme in Hubmaier's writings. According to Pipkin, it was an issue for Hubmaier largely because Zwingli makes it a significant issue. Hubmaier believes that John's baptism was a pre-resurrection baptism different from the baptism of Christ and the apostles, Hubmaier, "Christian Baptism," 103; Hubmaier, "Schriften," 125. What is important in John's baptism is the order and the nature of the response of the baptizand in relation to the act of baptism itself. A study of the biblical passages on the baptism of John, according to Pipkin's assessment of Hubmaier thought, is designed to prove the following order: (1) word, (2) hearing, (3) change of life or recognition of sin, (4) baptism, and (5) works. For more on Pipkin's understanding of Hubmaier's doctrine of the baptism of John, see Pipkin, "The Baptismal Theology".

93. Mabry, *Doctrine of the Church*, 138.

phenomenon of Spirit baptism: "in order to manifest to other believers in Christ his heart, mind, faith, and intention, he joins their brotherhood and churches, . . . [and] accepts and gives a public testimony of his internal faith and lets himself be baptized with water."[94]

Baptism, in Hubmaier's thought, then, was the way in which a regenerated person could testify to the reality of his faith and the authenticity of his inner regeneration to the church, which cannot see into his heart. In his commentary on Hubmaier's *Summa of the Entire Christian Life*, Christof Windhorst describes the Anabaptist's concept of water baptism as the "visible beginning of this new life in energetic love."[95] Hubmaier expounds this idea in his *Summa of the Entire Christian Life*: "After the person has now committed himself inwardly and in faith to a new life, he then professes this also outwardly and publicly before the Christian church, . . . [by letting himself] be baptized with outward water in which he professes publicly his faith and his intention."[96]

That water baptism was a serious commitment in Hubmaier's theology can be seen from the fact that it required a degree of preparation, theological awareness, and practical holiness, all of which was assessed by the bishop prior to presenting one to the church for approval. Littell's comment regarding the Anabaptist preparation for baptism is descriptive of Hubmaier's thought and practice: "The Anabaptists noted that the Master worked long with a small group, and then one of them betrayed Him. A long time of training was required for membership in the Early Church, and the True Church of the Restitution would not add members promiscuously."[97]

Hubmaier states in his *A Form for Water Baptism* that "Whoever desires water baptism should first present himself to his bishop, that he may be questioned, whether he is sufficiently instructed in the articles of the law, gospel, faith, and the doctrines which concern a new Christian life."[98]

The significance of baptism itself, according to Hubmaier, was in the fact that it encapsulated a great degree of theology with which a new church member would be in agreement and which he would proclaim by

---

94. Hubmaier, "Christian Baptism," 117; Hubmaier, "Schriften," 136.

95. "Die Taufe ist der sichtbare Beginn dieses neuen Lebens in tatkräftiger Liebe," Windhorst, *Täferisches Taufverständnis*, 31.

96. Hubmaier, "Summa," 85; Hubmaier, "Schriften," 111–12.

97. Littell, *The Anabaptist View of the Church*, 85.

98. Hubmaier, "A Form for Water Baptism," 387; Hubmaier, "Schriften," 349.

his participation in this ordinance. The first and most important reason for water baptism, according to Hubmaier, was because Christ had commanded it. What Christ has commanded should be gladly done by one who is truly regenerated.[99] As Hubmaier wrote, "all those who want to be considered Christians should let themselves be baptized according to the command of Christ and confess Christian faith publicly before the church with mouth and water, or they are looseners of his words."[100]

Second, water baptism for Hubmaier was a confession of sins.[101] Since by outer water baptism one publicly confesses inner faith, the first part of that confession is the recognition that one is a sinner.[102] Third, water baptism for Hubmaier, in the words of Mabry, is also "a witness to one's faith in the fact that following forgiveness, one has been reconciled to God."[103] "Baptism in the water . . . is nothing other than a public confession . . . by which the person . . . confesses himself guilty . . . yet at the same time he wholly believes that Christ has forgiven him his sin through his death and has made him righteous through his resurrection before the face of God our heavenly Father."[104]

Fourth, water baptism, in Hubmaier's writings, is the sign of the newly regenerated person's incorporation into the community of the saints.[105] The Radical Reformer explains in his Catechism that after one's public confession of sins and their forgiveness, the believer "has himself outwardly enrolled, inscribed, and by water baptism incorporated into the fellowship of the church according to the institution of Christ."[106] This act of incorporation then is a conscious decision made by the new believer and communicated to the local church, where the baptizand is not a passive participant but an active pursuer of the incorporation. Hubmaier's water baptism, therefore, when it is actively pursued by one fully cognizant of what it means, is designed to allow more accountability for the new believer before the church.

99. Mabry, *Doctrine of the Church*, 147.
100. Hubmaier, "On Infant Baptism," 292; Hubmaier, "Schriften," 268.
101. Mabry, *Doctrine of the Church*, 139.
102. Ibid.
103. Ibid., 140.
104. Hubmaier, "Christian Baptism," 100; Hubmaier, "Schriften," 122.
105. Mabry, *Doctrine of the Church*, 140.
106. Hubmaier, "Catechism," 349; Hubmaier, "Schriften," 314.

Fifth, water baptism, according to Hubmaier, then is a public commitment and agreement to a covenant which the new believer makes with God and before the church promising to live the life of active growth in progressive sanctification. Armour's research confirms this idea stating that "Hubmaier viewed baptism as the individual's own pledge of faithfulness and obedience to Christ, a pledge given within the Christian *Gemeinde* but made by the individual."[107] Hubmaier writes of the person who is incorporated into the church through water baptism that in the ordinance the same also "publicly and orally vows to God and agrees in the strength of God the Father, Son, and Holy Spirit that he will henceforth believe and live according to his divine Word."[108] Thus, baptism was a pledge that the new believer made to the church to live a holy life, which included in it therefore, permission for the church to discipline him, should he stray from this intent. In Hubmaier's own words, baptismal vow "is a commitment made to God publicly and orally before the congregation in which the baptized person renounces Satan and all his imaginations and works. He also vows that he will henceforth set his faith, hope, and trust solely in God and regulate his life according to the divine Word, in the strength of Jesus Christ our Lord, and if he should fail to do so, he thereby promises the church that he would dutifully accept brotherly discipline from it and its members."[109]

Estep summarizes the idea of the quote above quite aptly, stating that "baptism, was not, then, for Hübmaier simply an individual matter by which a man declares his faith. It is also a symbol of his submission to the discipline of the congregation to which he adheres and a prerequisite to the Lord's Supper."[110]

THE IMPORT OF CHURCH DISCIPLINE TO HUBMAIER'S VIEW OF WATER BAPTISM

Realizing the potentially unpleasant and difficult perspective of exercising church discipline for both the church and the straying member, Hubmaier's wisdom and forethought can be seen in his incorporation

---

107. Armour, *Anabaptist Baptism*, 40.
108. Hubmaier, "Catechism," 349; Hubmaier, "Schriften," 314.
109. Hubmaier, "Catechism," 350–51; Hubmaier, "Schriften," 314–15.
110. Estep, *Anabaptist Story*, 153.

of the doctrine of church discipline into water baptism. In building the acquiescence to be disciplined into the baptismal vow, Hubmaier's theology eliminates, or at least greatly lessens the awkwardness and vicissitude associated with the implementation of church discipline, should it ever be necessary.

The doctrine of church discipline, therefore, was key to Hubmaier's ordinance of baptism because it set in motion the plan to protect the purity of one's commitment made at baptism and to keep the overall church body unstained by the world. The understanding of and the ascent to the unique role of church discipline in Hubmaier's baptism provided a built-in aid to the spiritual maturation process of new believers in the reformer's ecclesiology. Without church discipline, Hubmaier's water baptism would not have differed much in its effectiveness for sanctification, from that of the Magisterial Reformers.

Furthermore, it is Hubmaier's understanding of church discipline and the unique role afforded to it in his overall theology that enabled him to connect every area of his theology to the practice of discipleship as the overarching theme of Anabaptism. Harold S. Bender, one of the foremost researchers of Anabaptist thought in the first part of the twentieth century, identifies this notion of discipleship as "the most characteristic, most central, most essential and regulative concept in Anabaptist thought, which largely determines all else."[111] Church discipline, therefore, functioned as a link for Hubmaier between the theoretical and practical sides of the various areas of theology. In other words, the doctrine of church discipline "practicalized," so to say, the otherwise seemingly theoretical doctrines within the Radical's theology.

Drawing from the reformer's *A Brief Apologia*, Williams summarizes cogently Hubmaier's perception of the three baptisms: "Hubmaier understood that Spirit baptism was the action of regeneration. Water baptism, a work of obedience to the Dominical command, introduced one to the church and served as external pledge of the inner decision of the will and movement of the Spirit. Following these, the baptism of blood was both encountered in the call to suffering and to inner mortification of the flesh, perhaps to death by martyrdom, in imitation of Christ."[112]

---

111. Harold Stauffer Bender, "The Anabaptist Theology of Discipleship," 27.

112. Williams, *The Radical Reformation*, 442 summarizing Hubmaier, "A Brief Apologia," 301; Hubmaier, "Schriften," 275.

In concluding the discussion of Hubmaier's understanding of water baptism, it is necessary to address a couple of misconceptions of the Radical Reformer's theology. First, Eddie Mabry, in his 1982 dissertation entitled "The Baptismal Theology of Balthasar Hubmaier," which was self-published in 1994 under the title *Balthasar Hubmaier's Doctrine of the Church*, makes the following summation of Hubmaier's baptismal understanding: "Water baptism, which is in obedience to the command of Christ, as well as the means by which one confesses his or her faith and is incorporated into the church is, according to Hubmaier, absolutely necessary for salvation."[113] In stating this, Mabry mirrors Christof Winhorst's assertion made in the previous decade. Windhorst wrote in his critical assessment of Hubmaier's *The Ground and Reason* that according to the reformer "church baptism is necessary for salvation because salvation of men depends on the church and its power of the keys."[114] Mabry uses a text from Hubmaier's *Dialogue With Oecolampad on Infant Baptism* in an attempt to prove this allegation: "Therefore all those who want to be considered Christians should let themselves be baptized according to the command of Christ and confess Christian faith publicly before the church with mouth and water, or they are looseners of his words."[115]

There are several reasons why Mabry's, and by extension Windhorst's assessment of the relation between water baptism and salvation in Hubmaier's theology is not accurate. First, by cutting off Hubmaier's quotation at this particular place, Mabry attempted to convey the idea that by the "looseners" of God's words, Hubmaier designates the unsaved. This, however, is not so. The next sentence in Hubmaier's aforementioned treatise makes it plain that such was not the reformer's understanding: "For whoever now loosens the smallest of his commandments will be called the smallest in the kingdom of God, Matt 5:19."[116] Mabry's chosen prooftext from Hubmaier then, does not support his assertion, for Hubmaier is not speaking here of salvation. Even if Hubmaier's above-mentioned statement concerned salvation, however, Mabry's claim would still be inaccurate for the following reason. This, incidentally, is also the reason

---

113. Mabry, *Doctrine of the Church*, 147.

114. "Die kirchliche Taufe ist heilsnotwendig, weil das Heil des Menschen von der Kirche und ihrer Schlüsselgewalt abhängig ist," Windhorst, *Täferisches Taufverständnis*, 128.

115. Hubmaier, "On Infant Baptism," 292; Hubmaier, "Schriften," 268.

116. Hubmaier, "On Infant Baptism," 292; Hubmaier, "Schriften," 268.

why Windhorst's assertion does not represent as faultless a depiction of Hubmaier's theology as it has been perceived thus far.[117] As pointed out in the previous chapter, Hubmaier's understanding of salvation was broader than just the salvific transaction and included sanctification as well. As such, since obedience to the Word of God is absolutely necessary to one's growth in sanctification, to say that for Hubmaier baptism is necessary for salvation, meaning sanctification, would be accurate, but without implying the idea that Hubmaier held to baptismal regeneration.[118]

William Estep is correct in claiming that "no one can successfully accuse Hübmaier of holding a sacramental view of baptism."[119] In his work, *The Anabaptist Story*, Estep provides a cogent explanation for why Hubmaier's understanding of baptism, and the Lord's Supper by extension, cannot be considered sacramental.[120]

---

117. The comprehensive nature of Windhorst's work would demand a similarly comprehensive research dedicated to interacting with and refuting his misconceptions, where necessary. As this lies outside of the scope of the present work, the direction of this research limits my interaction with Windhorst to passing comments. It is my opinion, however, that the time has come to interact more deeply and critically with Windhorst's seminal research than has been done up to this point.

118. More recently, Kirk MacGregor communicated basically the same idea as Mabry, but even more explicitly. In the 2006 self-published manuscript (MacGregor, *European Synthesis*) of his 2005 dissertation with a telling title of "The Sacramental Theology of Balthasar Hubmaier and Its Implications for Ecclesiology," MacGregor claims that Hubmaier championed the doctrine of baptismal regeneration. As the foregoing discussion of Hubmaier's baptismal understanding and the refutation of the previous error made it clear, however, this was not so. While the focus of this work does not permit the full refutation of MacGregor's premise here, pointing out an overall flaw in his argument should suffice. MacGregor's thesis depends largely on proving Hubmaier's literary dependence upon Bernard of Clairvaux. This he does not quite accomplish, however, lacking persuasiveness from the outset, as his only proof of Hubmaier's literary dependence upon Bernard of Clairvaux comes from one explicit reference to the latter's sermon entitled "On the Second Baptism" in the former's *A Simple Instruction*. From that point on the objectivity of MacGregor's methodology comes under serious suspicion, as both his choice of Hubmaier's works and his interpretation of the selected texts seems generally influenced by the theological bent of the twelfth-century monastic reformer. MacGregor seems more interested to find specific "proof texts" within Hubmaier's writings that affirm his own presupposition than to pay attention to the overall tenor of the reformer's theology of ordinances. MacGregor's evaluation of Hubmaier's understanding of ordinances, therefore, must be rejected as insufficiently grounded and misrepresenting the Radical Reformer's true position.

119. Estep, *Anabaptist Story*, 151–52.

120. Ibid.

John Rempel's dictum serves as an appropriate corrective to Windhorst, Mabry, MacGregor, and all the theologians before and after them, whose interpretation of Hubmaier seems to place extensive emphasis on the human participation in one's spiritual advancement. According to Rempel, "Hubmaier's pneumatology safeguards the work of grace in relation to an anthropology, ecclesiology, and Christology in which human response rather than divine initiative is emphasized."[121] In this author's opinion, the means by which this "safeguarding" is accomplished within Hubmaier's writings is his church discipline. In Hubmaier's soteriology, however, his doctrine of church discipline safeguards the work of grace in a more direct fashion.

The reason that Rempel identifies Hubmaier's pneumatology as a safeguard of the work of grace is because of the nuance in the reformer's Christology which will be discussed in more detail in the next section. According to Hubmaier, Christ is absent from history following his ascension. During Christ's absence the church acts in his stead as the outward expression of the Spirit's inward movement.[122] It is the church, therefore, that is the real presence of Christ's humanity on earth.[123] Proper understanding of this nuance in the Radical's theology enables one not to get bogged down in the dualism within the material world which characterizes Hubmaier's thought. Rempel identifies and deciphers the apparent dualism quite proficiently:

> in *Bann*, he [Hubmaier] has claimed that baptism is the first key of the church. By means of it, the church admits the believer to itself and to the forgiveness of sins. Further down, he emphasizes the role of the visible church as the mediator of Christ's power to forgive sins. The claim made by Hubmaier about the dominical ceremonies—that nothing outward can save—stands in complete contrast to the calling of the church, a visible, historical institution, which admits people to the forgiveness of sins.[124]

Rempel points out that "this dualism can exist within Hubmaier's thought because the church, in his view of it, is composed only of believers

---

121. "Everything salvific is the work of the Spirit," explains Rempel. "Even the symbolic role of Hubmaier's ceremonies is meaningless unless it is clear that they point to the life-giving work of the Spirit which precedes them." See Rempel, *The Supper*, 57.

122. Rempel, ibid., 83.

123. Ibid.

124. Ibid.

who collectively and individually bear the Spirit as well as the commission of Christ."[125] Unawareness or improper understanding of this dualism within Hubmaier's thought results in inaccurate interpretation of his theology as being heavily or even partially "works oriented," as was the case above with Windhorst, Mabry and MacGregor.[126]

LORD'S SUPPER

When it came to the Lord's Supper, Hubmaier's understanding was typical of the common Anabaptist perception of his day. Most Anabaptists rejected both the Catholic idea of transubstantiation[127] and the more "modest claims of the Supper as a sacrament in the Lutheran or Calvinist sense."[128] Christ's actual body and blood could not have possibly been in the elements themselves, according to the Waldshut reformer, since Christ had ascended to heaven and even now sits at the right hand of God the Father.[129] The risen Christ, in Hubmaier's theology, is currently limited to only one location, which is the right hand of the Father. This interpretation of Christology, while ignoring Luther's doctrine of the ubiquity of Christ and his ability to be omnipresent, was what allowed Hubmaier to combat the idea of the physical presence of Christ in the elements of the Lord's Supper. Yet to say simply that Hubmaier was not aware of Christ's ability to be omnipresent, as is implied and dutifully corrected, for example, in Mabry's work,[130] is to underestimate the reformer. Rempel ably corrects this oversimplification of Hubmaier's thought by stating that "though Hubmaier nowhere denies the presence of Christ in his divine nature in the ongoing course of history, he makes no use of this dogma in constructing his theology of the Lord's Supper."[131] With this

---

125. Ibid.

126. Rollin S. Armour can be added to the list as well, as he improperly understood Hubmaier's baptism as necessary for one's salvation, Armour, *Anabaptist Baptism*, 45–57.

127. The elements were transformed into Christ's literal flesh and blood at the moment of the priest's blessing of them. Consistent with this doctrine was the understanding that partaking of the elements was a necessary means for securing forgiveness of sin.

128. Rempel, *The Supper*, 63.

129. Mabry, *Doctrine of the Church*, 170.

130. Ibid., 170–71.

131. Rempel, *The Supper*, 54.

perspective in mind, the following statement of Hubmaier, in *A Form for Christ's Supper* can be properly appreciated:

> Although the majority of people who stand by the gospel recognize that bread is bread and wine wine in the Lord's Supper, and not Christ. For the same ascended into heaven and is sitting at the right hand of God his Father, whence he will come again to judge the living and the dead. Precisely that is our foundation, according to which we must deduce and exposit all of the Scriptures having to do with eating and drinking. Thus Christ cannot be eaten or drunk by us otherwise than spiritually and in faith. So then he cannot be bodily the bread either but rather in the memorial which is held, as he himself and Paul explained these Scriptures.[132]

It is the Holy Spirit that takes the prominent role as the medium of God's presence in the church, according to Hubmaier, after Christ's ascension. As relates to the Lord's Supper, Hubmaier maintained that Christ was present only with the believer in the Communion through memory.[133]

Like baptism, the Lord's Supper, according to Hubmaier, contained theological significance which had to be properly taught and explained to the participants. The Radical's desire to ground his theology in Scripture resulted in a carefully outlined script of how the believers were to be instructed prior to their participation in the Communion. At the outset of the service, the priest was to sit down and teach the people from Scripture about Christ, his death and suffering, and how it related to their lives.[134] To ensure that church members understood properly the meaning of the Supper and the serious nature of their willing participation in it, Hubmaier designed a time of discussion following the teaching time. Here the opportunity was presented within some specific parameters[135] for the males in the church to ask questions regarding the previous teaching.[136]

---

132. Hubmaier, "A Form for Supper," 407; Hubmaier, "Schriften," 364.

133. Mabry, *Doctrine of the Church*, 172.

134. Hubmaier, "A Form for Supper," 394–95; Hubmaier, "Schriften," 356.

135. Excluding "frivolous, unprofitable, or argumentative chatter," as well as things pertaining to "the omnipotence or the mystery of God or future things." All was to be done in an orderly manner, where people would take turns to speak. In accordance with the Pauline instruction of 1 Cor 11 and 14, women were to keep silence in the congregation, addressing their questions to their husbands at home. See Hubmaier, "A Form for Supper," 395–96; Hubmaier, "Schriften," 356.

136. Hubmaier, "A Form for Supper," 395–96; Hubmaier, "Schriften," 356.

Church Discipline and Ecclesiology 109

Finally, a time of self-examination was established by Hubmaier before the actual participation in the Supper. Following the priest's stern admonishment based on the Pauline warning in 1 Cor 11, the believers participating in the Supper were to examine themselves in the following areas. First, they were to make sure that they believed "utterly and absolutely" that Christ died for them.[137] Second, the believers were to make certain that they not only knew Christ as their Savior, but were in fellowship with him. Hubmaier expressed it quite beautifully: "Let a person test himself, whether he has a proper inward and fervent hunger for the bread which comes down from heaven, from which one truly lives, and thirst for the drink which flows into eternal life, to eat and drink both in the spirit, faith and truth, as Christ teaches us in John 4; 6; and 7. If the spiritual eating and drinking does not first take place, then the outward breaking of bread, eating and drinking is a killing letter."[138]

Third, upon examining their relationship and fellowship with their Savior, the believers were to test their willingness and readiness to do for the Lord as he had done for them. This desire to give back to the Lord would flow from their gratitude "for the great, overabundant, and unspeakable love and goodness that he [God] has shown him [the believer] through his most beloved Son, our Lord Jesus Christ."[139] And since the Lord "does not need our good deeds," the believers that are ready to partake of the Communion, would be ready to fulfill these works of gratitude towards their fellow believers, "physically and spiritually, feeding the hungry, giving drink to the thirsty, clothing the naked, consoling the prisoner, sheltering the needy."[140] Fourth, in preparation for the Lord's Supper, church members were to assess their volition and preparedness to offer their bodies and to shed their blood for their fellow believers. Thus, in the words of Rempel, "Christ's sacrifice for humanity becomes the transforming power of history when those who claim it imitate its sacrifice."[141] According to Hubmaier, this readiness of the believer was not to be ascertained based on his human ability or "human daring, like Peter, but in the grace and power of the suffering and the blood shed by

---

137. Hubmaier, "A Form for Supper," 396; Hubmaier, "Schriften," 357.
138. Hubmaier, "A Form for Supper," 396–97; Hubmaier, "Schriften," 357.
139. Hubmaier, "A Form for Supper," 397; Hubmaier, "Schriften," 357.
140. Hubmaier, "A Form for Supper," 397; Hubmaier, "Schriften," 357.
141. Rempel, *The Supper*, 70.

our Lord Jesus Christ, his (i.e., meaning Peter's) only Savior, of whose suffering and death the human being is now celebrating a living commemoration in the breaking of bread and the sharing of the chalice."[142]

Following this extensive preparation for the Supper, the believers were allowed to participate in the sacred meal.[143] Their participation in the Communion, as mentioned earlier, was a *de facto* affirmation of some important theological points according to Hubmaier's understanding of this ordinance. First, the Lord's Supper for Hubmaier, much like the case of water baptism, did not convey grace, but was a memorial of the suffering of Christ.[144] Believers were to be reminded of that, according to Hubmaier's *A Form for Christ's Supper*, where at the conclusion of the meal, the priest was to proclaim the following statement: "Most dearly beloved brethren and sisters in the Lord. As we now, by thus eating the bread and drinking the drink in memory of the suffering and shed blood of our Lord Jesus Christ for the remission of our sins have had fellowship one with another."[145] Through remembering, the believers would partake in Christ's suffering and be reminded of their commitment, made at baptism, to live a saintly life.

Second, as the memorial of Christ's suffering, according to Hubmaier, the Lord's Supper was also an affirmation or witness on the part of believers of their readiness to offer their bodies and pour out their blood for the sake of their brothers and sisters. During the time of self-examination, they tested their readiness to do so and now they had the opportunity to proclaim this preparedness boldly through the Supper. The Lord's Supper, therefore, is not only a memorial of Christ's gift of life for the believers, but also a commitment to practice active fellowship to the point of sacrificing their lives for the sake of the community of faith. In his monumental study of the Radical Reformation, Williams notes that, in Hubmaier's theology "as believers' baptism is a pledge to Christ, so the Supper is a mutual pledge, one to another."[146] Continuing his charge at the conclusion of the Supper, the officiating priest would remind all gathered, in Hubmaier's *A Form for Christ's Supper* of the commitment that they had

142. Hubmaier, "A Form for Supper," 398; Hubmaier, "Schriften," 358.

143. For a more thorough and extensive treatment of Hubmaier's liturgical celebration of the Lord's Supper, see Rempel, *The Supper*, 74–78.

144. Mabry, *Doctrine of the Church*, 166.

145. Hubmaier, "A Form for Supper," 405; Hubmaier, "Schriften," 363.

146. Williams, *The Radical Reformation*, 337.

Church Discipline and Ecclesiology

just reaffirmed by their participation in the Communion: "As we now, by thus eating the bread and drinking the drink in memory of the suffering and shed blood of our Lord Jesus Christ . . . have all become one loaf and one body, and our Head is Christ, we should properly become conformed to our Head and as his members follow after him, love one another, do good, give counsel, and be helpful to one another, each offering up his flesh and blood for the other."[147]

With this pledge of commitment to sacrifice one's life for the sake of fellow believers, Hubmaier, according to Rempel's assessment, made his theology of the Lord's Supper "adequate to the needs of a persecuted church threatened with martyrdom."[148] Rempel further pointed out that this particular eucharistic teaching of Hubmaier's did not only "help beleaguered Christians find meaning in their circumstances; it also prepared them to be loyal to Christ until death."[149]

Third, the Lord's Supper, in Hubmaier's writings, served as a public testimony to the world that those who partook of it were truly Christ's disciples.[150] The Radical Reformer pointed out in *A Form for Christ's Supper*: "It is precisely to this fellowship and commitment of love that the Supper of Christ points, as a living memorial of his suffering and death for us, spiritually signified and pointed to by the breaking of bread, the pouring out of the wine, that each one should also sacrifice and pour out his flesh and blood for the other. Herein will people recognize that we are truly disciples of Christ."[151]

Thus for Hubmaier, the Lord's Supper was the visual reminder of the covenant into which one entered at baptism. This covenant, which was first between the church member and God, was a commitment made at baptism to love, honor, and serve God subjecting oneself to his will according to his Word.[152] Second, the baptismal covenant, of which the Supper served as a reminder, was also between the new member and the church. To the church the new member committed at baptism to love his fellow believers and to be willing and ready to shed his blood for their

---

147. Hubmaier, "A Form for Supper," 405; Hubmaier, "Schriften," 363.
148. Rempel, *The Supper*, 88.
149. Ibid.
150. Mabry, *Doctrine of the Church*, 167.
151. Hubmaier, "A Form for Supper," 398–99; Hubmaier, "Schriften," 358.
152. Mabry, *Doctrine of the Church*, 168.

sake.[153] Third, the Lord's Supper was both a reminder and a reaffirmation of the permission given at baptism to be disciplined by the church, should the new believer not live up to the first two commitments.

THE IMPORT OF CHURCH DISCIPLINE TO HUBMAIER'S VIEW OF THE LORD'S SUPPER

Thus the subject of church discipline emerges to the prominent place within the reformer's understanding not only of baptism but also of the Lord's Supper. In the actual service where the Lord's Supper is celebrated, according to *A Form for Christ's Supper*, after extensive preparation during the service and prior to partaking of the meal, the believer makes a pledge of love in which he explicitly states his commitment to "practice fraternal admonition" toward his brothers and sisters: "If you will practice fraternal admonition toward your brethren and sisters, make peace and unity among them, and reconcile yourselves with all those whom you have offended, abandon all envy, hate, and evil will toward everyone, willingly cease all action and behavior which causes harm, disadvantage, or offense to your neighbor, [if you will] also love your enemies and do good to them, and exclude according to the Rule of Christ, all those who refuse to do so, then let each say individually: I will."[154]

It is assumed, therefore, that those who agree to practice admonition, or discipline are also authorizing their fellow believers to exercise church discipline in their lives, should it be warranted. Rempel correctly analyzes the ethical elements of commitment and discipline in Hubmaier's Communion: "In a strange way the ethical nagging in which Hubmaier gets caught up is the highest tribute he can pay to the Lord's Supper. In it the believer speaks the word of promise to live a life of love. Therefore, unbelievers can rightly judge their faith

and their love by how Christians live. Because their lives are the book which the world reads, believers must discipline each other in love."[155]

The intersection between the Lord's Supper and church discipline, however, does not stop there. For, after partaking of the elements, every time that the Lord's Supper is administered, believers are reminded by

---

153. Ibid.
154. Hubmaier, "A Form for Supper," 403; Hubmaier, "Schriften," 362.
155. Rempel, *The Supper*, 78.

Church Discipline and Ecclesiology 113

the priest of the steps to church discipline delineated in Matt 18.[156] The Communion is to end with the following charge from the presiding minister: "Be mindful of your baptismal commitment and of your pledge of love which you made to God and the church publicly and certainly not unwittingly when receiving the water and in breaking bread."[157]

Consequently, in addition to what was already stated above, the following points of intersection between the Lord's Supper and church discipline identify the latter as an indispensable element in the practice of the former. First, church discipline is essential to maintaining the community of the Supper by providing a reminder to the participants of their baptismal vows. The Lord's Supper, as was demonstrated in this work, was the ordinance that necessitated the context of community for its celebration. This community, as was also pointed out previously, had to be in fellowship with God and one another in order to participate in Communion. It was Hubmaier's construct of church discipline at the center of his understanding of the Lord's Supper, therefore, that assured the congregation's readiness and ability to partake of Communion on any given day. For as often as the Lord's Supper is celebrated, believers are reminded of the commitment that they made in their baptism, which included permission to be disciplined by the church, and affirmed their continued willingness to be held accountable by their brothers and sisters. The subject of church discipline is continually refreshed in the minds and hearts of these believers as they constantly reaffirm their commitment to a lifestyle of transparency and accountability. Mabry's summation of Hubmaier's Supper is correct when he states that it was "more than just a memorial of Christ's death (as in the case of the Anabaptists), but it was also a comprehensive covenant which included the whole of one's life and activities."[158]

Second, church discipline in close association with the Lord's Supper was an important instrument for one's progressive sanctification. Given the import of the Lord's Supper to one's growth and progression in the process of sanctification within Hubmaier's theology, the intimate interrelation between Communion and church discipline is of particular significance. For the close connection between these two doctrines enabled the reformer to provide the church with a mechanism to encourage the

---

156. Hubmaier, "A Form for Supper," 406; Hubmaier, "Schriften," 364.
157. Hubmaier, "A Form for Supper," 406; Hubmaier, "Schriften," 364.
158. Mabry, *Doctrine of the Church*, 168.

desire within the straying believer to return to the safety and security of the fold of God. Robert Friedmann's comment regarding the Anabaptist view of church discipline via separation from the Lord's Supper converges with this author's assessment of Hubmaier's understanding: "to them the ban was nothing but the practice of a form of brotherly love to help the one who went astray to find his way back into the holy community. Discipline assumed a redemptive quality besides its primary cathartic function."[159] In such context church discipline did, in fact, assume the true function of a "healing plaster" within the church, as Hubmaier himself once called it.[160] Away from the fold and unable to partake of the Supper, in the case of the ban, the person has been put out from the life of the community, and has no access to its instructions and support, its nurturing to righteousness and its protection.[161]

Third, church disciplined within the context of the Lord's Supper helped outline the parameters of Hubmaier's community of faith. Commenting on the communal aspect of the Anabaptist piety, which was true also of Hubmaier's understanding, Nigel Wright pointed out that "piety was not to be pursued or expressed in individualism or isolation but communally, so that communion, footwashing, singing, and corporate prayer should be seen as indispensable aspects of Anabaptist spirituality."[162] If Wright's comments could be applied to Hubmaier's theological understanding of the Lord's Supper and the Lord's Supper was indeed an indispensable aspect of Hubmaier's conception of spirituality, then church discipline, as the element that outlined the parameters of the community, had to lie at the center of his theology of the Communion.

In his article "No Discipline, No Church: An Anabaptist Contribution to the Reformed Tradition," Kenneth R. Davis succinctly concludes the import of church discipline to the Anabaptist, and by extension Hubmaier's, doctrine of the Lord's Supper, writing "without the ban even the Supper (as also a pledge of love requiring a true perception

---

159. Friedmann, *The Theology of Anabaptism*, 122.

160. A marginal gloss in Hubmaier, "Schriften," 343, reading: "Die Brüederlich straff ist ein hailsam pflaster."

161. Mabry, *Doctrine of the Church*, 176; Hubmaier, "Ban," 416–25; Hubmaier, "Schriften," 372–77.

162. Wright, "Spirituality as Discipleship: The Anabaptist Heritage," 87.

of the Lord's body, the church) would be destroyed, and all eating and drinking became condemnatory."[163]

As for those who, like MacGregor, ascribe sacramental value, in full Catholic meaning of the term, to Hubmaier's understanding of the Lord's Supper, such views demonstrate a misunderstanding of the Radical Reformer's overall theological dictum.[164] Since full-fledged refutation of such misunderstanding lies outside of the boundaries of the present research, the reader should be pointed first to the concluding remarks of the previous section on water baptism. In addition to refuting such claims, the aforementioned section contains suggestions for further resources that provide a more wholistic understanding of the thought of Balthasar Hubmaier.

This chapter set out to examine the relation between Hubmaier's doctrine of the ordinances and his understanding of church discipline. In the process of the examination, it became evident that, in the words of H. Wayne Pipkin, Hubmaier is "joining very closely the three concerns of baptism, fraternal admonition, and the Supper as a sacramental matrix expressing the whole of the Christian life."[165] Pipkin's assessment, while accurate on its own, also confirms the claim laid at the outset of the present chapter, namely that church discipline was absolutely essential to Hubmaier's theology of the ordinances of baptism and the Lord's Supper.

---

163. Davis, "No Discipline, No Church," 47–48.

164. He states that "Contrary to the widespread view that Hubmaier, like his supposed Anabaptist brethren, rejected the application of the term 'sacrament' to the Lord's Supper, an examination of the reformer's three treatises on the subject along with many of his other writings reveal that Hubmaier displayed no qualms in . . . assigning sacramental nomenclature to the Eucharist." See MacGregor, *European Synthesis*, 183.

165. Pipkin, "The Baptismal Theology," 90.

5

Conclusion

Although the name of Balthasar Hubmaier may not be as well-known today as those of Martin Luther, John Calvin, or even Ulrich Zwingli, such was not the case four centuries ago. In the first part of the sixteenth century, the Anabaptist leader was as widely known in southern Germany, Austria, and Moravia as were Luther and Zwingli. According to Robert A. Macoskey, "in some areas he [Hubmaier] was considered more important to the evangelical aspiration and more dangerous to the entrenched religious powers" than aforementioned reformers.[1] Condemnation of the Catholic Church, equal to that of Luther and Zwingli, was just one of the proofs to the effectiveness and relevance of the sixteenth-century Radical Reformer.[2]

As a "true Free Churchman,"[3] Balthasar Hubmaier was crucial to theological development of the free church of the present. His ideas were more anticipatory than normative and in Macoskey's accurate estimation, "had he survived the imperial fury, the course of the great Free Church tributary of the Reformation might well have been different."[4] Given the import of his theology, therefore, as well as this reformer's remarkably

---

1. Macoskey, "Hubmaier's Concept of the Church," 102.

2. In the official minutes of the censuring commission of the Council of Trent, Hubmaier's writings are placed by the side of Luther's and Zwingli's. Furthermore, Cardinal Bernhard of Sandoval in his index of forbidden books gives several variations of Hubmaier's name that there may be no doubt as to the identity of this heretical author. He is listed as "Balthasar Hiebmaier, Hilcemerus, Isbumarus, Pacimontanus," Macoskey, "Hubmaier's Concept of the Church," 102. See also Windhorst, "Hubmaier," 144.

3. Macoskey, "Hubmaier's Concept of the Church," 102.

4. Ibid.

understudied life, one cannot but agree with Robert Friedmann's opinion about the need for more research in the field of Hubmaier studies.[5] Although much has changed in the five decades since the time that Friedmann made his assessment, Friedmann's utterance still holds true today, as not much detailed investigation has been undertaken on the majority of Hubmaier's treatises. The goal of the present study, therefore, has been to contribute to Hubmaier research by offering a proper alignment of his theology in view of his central and underlying emphasis on the doctrine of church discipline.

The process of researching and compiling the data for this manuscript produced some interesting discoveries, which will be listed below in order of importance. The first discovery was of more personal nature. Many of the findings of the current research, including Hubmaier's anthropology (grounded in the doctrine of free will), his soteriology (with strong emphasis on sanctification), the ordinances (with a heavy leaning on commitment and pledge contained therein), and dedication to consistent practice of church discipline as the factor underlying all of the above, resonated with me by bringing to mind the traditions of my own childhood church. The reason for the similarities listed here is that my Russian Baptist church owes its origin to the German Mennonites, who trace their lineage to Menno Simons, one of the renown Anabaptist leaders of the sixteenth century.[6] These Anabaptist/Mennonite forefathers of the Russian Baptist church settled in southern Russia in the nineteenth century at the invitation of Catherine II.[7] In his article "Russian Mennonites and Baptists," Walter Sawatsky states, "The Russian evangelical movement that emerged in the second half of the nineteenth century was, to a great extent, the spiritual child of the pietistic German colonists in South Russia, including the Mennonites."[8]

Growing up with a Russian Baptist heritage gave me an "eye witness" account of the church heavily influenced by Anabaptist theology and practice. As a result, the subject at hand was both highly intriguing and very significant to me as one whose childhood church's Anabaptist beginnings add a certain personal dimension to the present work.

5. Friedmann, "A Bibliography of Anabaptism," 359.
6. Toews, "Baptists and Mennonites in Russia," 90.
7. Ibid., 87.
8. Sawatsky, "Russian Mennonites and Baptists," 113.

The second discovery establishes a significant corrective to the understanding of Hubmaier's thought. It was precipitated by the research of John Rempel and his 1993 work entitled *The Lord's Supper in Anabaptism*. Examining the ordinance of Communion in the writings of Hubmaier and Marpeck, Rempel dedicates some fifty pages to the former theologian. Nestled in these pages is the discussion of a certain dualism within Hubmaier's thought between the reformer's ardent denial of any external right containing salvific powers and his understanding of the church as the sole agency on this earth which admits people to the forgiveness of sins: "in *Bann*, he [Hubmaier] has claimed that baptism is the first key of the church. By means of it, the church admits the believer to itself and to the forgiveness of sins. Further down, he emphasizes the role of the visible church as the mediator of Christ's power to forgive sins. The claim made by Hubmaier about the dominical ceremonies—that nothing outward can save—stands in complete contrast to the calling of the church, a visible, historical institution, which admits people to the forgiveness of sins."[9]

Rempel further points out that "this dualism can exist within Hubmaier's thought because the church, in his view, is composed only of believers who collectively and individually bear the Spirit as well as the commission of Christ."[10] According to Rempel's accurate analysis, since Hubmaier views the church as the real presence of Christ's humanity on earth during the period following his ascension,[11] the Holy Spirit operating within believers "safeguards the work of grace in relation to an anthropology, ecclesiology, and Christology in which human response rather than divine initiative is emphasized."[12] This is the point where Rempel's research regarding the Holy Spirit's preservation of the work of grace in relation to Hubmaier's theology intersects the current focus—that being the importance of church discipline to Hubmaier's theology. For in my opinion, the Holy Spirit's work of "safeguarding" is accomplished *by means of church discipline*. Though the subject of pneumatological safeguarding lies outside the scope of the present work, what is significant for the purpose of this research is that the importance of Hubmaier's doctrine of church discipline is further exemplified in the fact

---

9. Rempel, *The Supper*, 83.
10. Ibid.
11. Ibid.
12. Ibid., 57.

that it was the means by which the Holy Spirit preserved the work of grace in relation to Hubmaier's theology.

A contemporary of the great reformer Martin Luther, Balthasar Hubmaier's unique background enabled him to evaluate critically all the contemporaneous branches of theology, from Catholic to Lutheran, to Reformed, to Anabaptist. His particular evaluation did not rest on the inherent logic within each system but on its adherence to the Word of God. It was God's Word, therefore, that propelled Balthasar Hubmaier to join the ranks of the Radical Reformation, of which he eventually became most renowned leader.

Aside from his theological divergence from Luther or Zwingli, it was Hubmaier's desire to unravel complicated doctrinal arguments for the layman that distinguished and endeared him to the average believer of his day. Numerous and significant changes in the theological arena of the sixteenth century produced a general bewilderment in the minds of common people. In the words of Macoskey, while "the leaders [of the Reformation] were finding answers, little light was filtering down to the people."[13]

Anyone familiar with the context of the Anabaptist reform of the sixteenth century is aware of the intense suffering and persecution that was faced by all who chose to submit to believer's baptism.[14] This period of indiscriminate suffering at the hands of the Roman Catholic Church as well as the churches of the Classical Reformation had its effect on the development of Anabaptist theology. As a result, much, if not most of Anabaptist theology, as is evidenced by the writings of Hubmaier, was of practical nature. Macoskey captures the essence of the practical bent of Hubmaier's theology as he succinctly expresses: "When people understood the naked truths of a vital faith, there would be time to put on the clothes of a systematic theology."[15] Accordingly, literary works penned during this period tended to address the issues of practical piety and specific application of the biblical doctrine. Little, if any time during this period was devoted to the development of systematic dogma, for such a luxury simply could not be afforded to the Radical Reformers.[16] Also,

13. Macoskey, "Hubmaier's Concept of the Church," 104.

14. The average life expectancy for an Anabaptist between his "legitimate" baptism (i.e., believer's baptism) and his martyr's death was eighteen months.

15. Macoskey, "Hubmaier's Concept of the Church," 105.

16. In Hubmaier's case, that he did not leave a large body of systematic theology was

influenced not only by outside persecutions but also, to a large extent, by their own doctrinal commitments, the understanding of and ardent devotion to the regular practice of church discipline, as has been made evident from Hubmaier's theology, seems to be a common characteristic of the Anabaptist reform.

The main element of the "doctrinal commitment" was the Anabaptist understanding of the church as a body of regenerated believers. Hubmaier, as perhaps one of the finest representatives of Anabaptist theology, did not share with Luther and the Reformed theologians the understanding of the church consisting of "wheat and tares." The purity of such congregations had to be maintained via church discipline, which was developed from the various texts of the New Testament, with Matt 18:15–22 as the most prominent one.

That the doctrine of church discipline was important to Hubmaier's theology as a whole can be seen clearly even from the fact that it is referenced in at least half of his treatises. It can be seen also from the convergence of the doctrine of church discipline with many, if not most, other doctrines in Hubmaier's theology, including his anthropology. Hubmaier's trichotomous understanding of the makeup of man, influenced as it was by his studies in medieval scholasticism and his interactions with contemporaneous Humanism, allowed him to hold to the freedom of the human will, where the spirit of man was unaffected by the fall of Adam. The aforementioned influences notwithstanding, however, it was Hubmaier's interpretation of Paul's writings as well as several other Scriptural references to man as consisting of spirit, soul, and body, that became the major impetus for his particular anthropology. When, following his Son's salvific mission on this earth, God the Father draws all men through his life-giving Word, which he speaks into people's hearts, according to Hubmaier, it is the freedom of the human will that enables people to respond in faith, if they so choose. This response in faith, however, cannot take place without the person first hearing the preached word or without

---

not a commentary on his ability to think or argue systematically. Macoskey correctly points out that in his university days, Hubmaier was trained "to confound debate opponents with every subtlety of dialectic. He would not have retained the leadership of the debate fraternity at the University of Freiburg if he had been inept at threading his way through elaborate philosophical and theological arguments." Macoskey, "Hubmaier's Concept of the Church," 105.

the Spirit's work in the hearts of men enlivening the preached word into the Word of God.

When it comes to the relation between church discipline and anthropology, it is Hubmaier's anthropological understanding of the trichotomous division of the nature of man that forms the basis for his pervasive doctrine of church discipline. Man's freedom of the will, a close corollary of Hubmaier's anthropology, drives the voluntary nature of church membership within the theology of the Anabaptist leader. Consistent within voluntary membership was the voluntary commitment and permission given at baptism to both participate in the exercise of church discipline and have it exercised in one's own life. Additionally, Hubmaier's church discipline enables his anthropology to contribute to the mutual process of accountability within a local church. Finally, it is Hubmaier's trichotomous understanding of the make up of man that allows him to keep perfect tension between the church's ability to execute eternal judgments on erring sinners and the believer's ability to retain his salvation. In commenting on the first Pauline letter to the church in Corinth where, in chapter 5, the Apostle commits the body of the incestuous man to Satan for the salvation of his spirit, Hubmaier believes that it is the *flesh* that is being punished by the ban. Consequently, in Hubmaier's view, even when repentance, as the desired product of the ban, never occurs on earth, the *spirit* of the believer, as the incorruptible part of him, would be preserved and saved. The reason for this is Hubmaier's understanding of the church currently possessing the keys of the kingdom which Christ handed to her upon his ascension and thus enables her to make decisions on earth, the majority of which will be upheld in heaven.[17] Resulting from such understanding of anthropology and ecclesiology, Hubmaier would hold, according to Klassen, that "Salvation is still a possibility for those outside the Church (the excommunicated or unevangelized) but not while they remain alive on earth."[18]

The doctrine of church discipline was integral to Hubmaier's understanding of the ordinances because of his association of the ordinances with the keys of the kingdom. As mentioned above, Hubmaier believed that the power of the keys, namely loosing and binding, was given by

17. The reason that not all the church's decisions would be upheld in heaven is because Hubmaier believed that while the universal / mother church was unable to err, such could not be said for the local / daughter church.

18. Klassen, "Two Swords," 65.

Christ to the church to be used through its exercise of church discipline in the context of the ordinances.

The ordinance of water baptism, which in Hubmaier's theology was preceded by the inner baptism of the Spirit and followed by the baptism of the blood, was described by MacGregor as the reformer's *sine qua non* of the church.[19] Believing that faith had to precede water baptism,[20] Hubmaier rejected the sacramental understanding present within the Catholic Church, reassigning the sacramental value of the act to the human commitment that was made while participating in it. As such, for Hubmaier, baptism was a human testimony to the reality of one's faith and the authenticity of that person's inner regeneration to the church, which cannot see into his heart. In addition to that, baptism was also a confession of sins,[21] a witness to one's reconciliation to God, a sign of the newly regenerated person's incorporation into the community of saints, and a public commitment and agreement to a covenant with God and before the church in which the new believer promises to live a life of active growth in progressive sanctification. Included in that covenant was the pledge made by the believer to participate in practicing church discipline in the life of the straying member of the congregation, as well as the acquiescence given by the believer to have it exercised in his own life, should it become necessary. The essential meaning of Hubmaier's baptism, therefore, is open confession, at the core of which lies the sole right to discipline and excommunicate.[22]

Consequently, church discipline was very important to Hubmaier's understanding of baptism because it set in motion the plan to protect the purity of one's baptismal commitment and to keep the overall church body unstained by the world. Perhaps most importantly, however, was the fact that it was Hubmaier's doctrine of church discipline, as interconnected with his doctrine of baptism, that enabled the Radical Reformer to connect every area of his theology to the practice of discipleship as the overarching theme of Anabaptism. Church discipline, therefore, functioned as a link for Hubmaier between the theoretical and practical sides of the various areas of theology.

19. MacGregor, *European Synthesis*, 152.

20. This belief was, in part, what forced Hubmaier to reject infant baptism as unbiblical and ineffective.

21. See chapter 4 for a more detailed explanation of this point.

22. Macoskey, "Hubmaier's Concept of the Church," 112, 115.

Hubmaier's understanding of the Lord's Supper, like baptism, excluded both the Catholic idea of transubstantiation and the more modest claims of Communion as a sacrament in the Lutheran or Calvinist sense.[23] While Macoskey is correct in that Hubmaier mainly "agrees with Zwingli and Karlstadt in viewing the ordinance as a memorial meal,"[24] the Lord's Supper is more than that for the Radical Reformer. Believing the Lord's Supper to be an important and theologically significant ordinance, Hubmaier dedicated a whole treatise to outlining carefully both the participation in the sacred meal, and the preparation leading up to it. According to Macoskey, participation in the Lord's Supper "completes the open confession of Baptism and carries with it the second significance, that of commission."[25] Through partaking of Communion the believer expresses his readiness to convey Christian love to his neighbor and thereby be a witness in accordance with Christ's commissioning.[26] Macoskey goes on to add that "the ordinances mean nothing at all unless both aspects of a true faith, i.e., confession and commission, are operating."[27]

Rather than conveying grace, the Lord's Supper for Hubmaier was first a memorial of the suffering of Christ; second, it was an affirmation or witness of the participants' readiness to offer their bodies and pour their blood for the sake of their brothers and sisters;[28] third, it was a public testimony of the fact that those who partook of it were truly Christ's disciples. Thus for Hubmaier, Communion was both a visual reminder of the covenant into which one entered at baptism and a reaffirmation of the permission given at baptism to be disciplined by the church, should the new believer not live up to the original commitment.

Here the subject of church discipline emerges again as integral to Hubmaier's understanding and practice of the Supper. For church discipline was essential to maintaining the community of the Lord's Supper by providing the aforementioned reminder to the participants of their baptismal vows. Additionally, church discipline, in its close association with the Supper, was an important instrument for one's progressive sanctification

23. Rempel, *The Supper*, 63.
24. Macoskey, "Hubmaier's Concept of the Church," 116.
25. Ibid., 113.
26. Ibid.
27. Ibid.
28. Macoskey calls this part a "love oath," Macoskey, "Hubmaier's Concept of the Church," 116.

by providing the church with a mechanism by which it could revive and encourage the desire within the straying believer to return to the spiritual safety and security of the fold of God. Kenneth R. Davis' comment succinctly summarizes the importance of church discipline to the Anabaptist, and by extension Hubmaier's, doctrine of the Lord's Supper: "without the ban even the Supper (as also a pledge of love requiring a true perception of the Lord's body, the church) would be destroyed, and all eating and drinking became condemnatory."[29]

Macoskey's apt depiction of the interrelation between Hubmaier's doctrines of church discipline and ecclesiology, particularly the ordinances and the keys of the kingdom, summarizes well the preceding discussion:

> How does Hübmaier relate discipline and punishment to the ordinances? Three of his emphases are important in this connection: 1.) the baptismal vow, 2.) the love oath sworn during the celebration of the Supper, and 3.) the church's power of the keys. The first two provide the basis upon which church discipline and punishment is established. By giving his vow, the believer freely agrees to better his life and place himself under the rule of Christ. Through the love oath, he swears to extend brotherly love and works of compassion to his neighbor. Trespass against either of these makes a person liable to Christian chastisement. The "power of the keys" provides an external and complementary justification for punishment. In other words, the vow and the oath are the means, the keys are the way.[30]

The third discovery is regarding Hubmaier's soteriology. The import of church discipline to the reformer's doctrine of salvation lies in the fact that it safeguards directly the work of grace in relation to Hubmaier's soteriology in which human response rather than divine initiative is emphasized. In other words, the role played by Hubmaier's doctrine of church discipline in his soteriology is what enables the Radical Reformer's understanding and exposition of salvation to not veer into "works-based" territory.

Human response to the preached Word is very important to Hubmaier's understanding of salvation. It is what separates him from both Lutheran and Reformed soteriological positions. Equally important

---

29. Davis, "No Discipline, No Church," 47–48.
30. Macoskey, "Hubmaier's Concept of the Church," 117.

to the Radical Reformer's soteriology is the life of righteousness or growth in discipleship after the salvific transaction. The whole idea of discipleship became the overarching theme of the Anabaptist soteriology. What safeguarded one's growth in discipleship or salvation process, to state it in Hubmaier's terminology, was his ardent commitment to and faithful practice of church discipline. Having spent a lifetime entrenched in Catholic theology, it is no surprise to find Hubmaier's theological nomenclature very Catholic-sounding although his understanding progressed far beyond his mother church. This explains how his doctrine of church discipline replaced the Roman idea of sacraments as important to Hubmaier's soteriology, though without containing salvific elements.[31] This was perhaps the most important discovery of the present work.

The unique nature of the Radical Reformer's soteriological understanding was established earlier in this work. It was neither Catholic nor Protestant, in the Lutheran or Reformed sense of that word. But it was grounded faithfully in his understanding and interpretation of the Scripture, most of which to this day stands uncontested and uncorrected.

Propelled by his anthropological commitment to the freedom of human will, Hubmaier was unwilling to accept the Magisterial Reformer's understanding of faith as simply a gift from God or ascribe to their understanding of the alien righteousness of man, imputed by Christ. Furthermore, unconvinced by Augustine's predestinarian tendencies present within the writings of Luther and Zwingli and expressed in their understanding of the irresistible grace, Hubmaier believed that faith, while enabled by God, was still a free response of man to the Holy Spirit's prompting.

Above all else, however, what doubtlessly set Hubmaier's soteriology apart from that of any other contemporaneous system was its monumental emphasis on discipleship, aided by church discipline. According to Cornelius J. Dyck, as mentioned before, Hubmaier and the Anabaptists held to the notion of discipleship in which "obedience was first of all a response of gratitude and identification with Christ."[32] Out of love for what

---

31. In considering Hubmaier's theology, one must not forget that the reformer spent thirty-nine years as a Roman Catholic teacher, priest, apologist, and crusader. Having devoted the last four years of his life to "the expurgation of those old influences," it is "neither remarkable nor a disgrace" that he may have failed to "purge every vestige of them," Macoskey, "Hubmaier's Concept of the Church," 106.

32. Dyck, "Life of the Spirit in Anabaptism," 317.

God had accomplished for him through Christ, the believer, in Hubmaier's soteriological understanding, had his righteousness restored to where he could, in fact, lead a life of progressive sanctification. This particular understanding of salvation resulted partially in response to the ethical consequences of the soteriological views of the Magisterial Reformers, which, in Hubmaier's opinion, lacked the desired moral fruits.[33] Incidentally, neither Hubmaier nor the vast majority of Anabaptists held to the possibility of attaining perfectionism, of which their highly developed doctrine of church discipline was a testimony.

Thus the doctrine of church discipline was relegated to the place of extreme import in Hubmaier's soteriology, much like the sacraments were for the Catholic dogma, but without depending on it for one's salvation. In fact, it was Hubmaier's doctrine of church discipline that caused him to reiterate on several occasions Cyprian's dictum of *Extra Ecclesiam Nulla Salus*, "no salvation outside the church." Whereas for both Cyprian and the medieval theologians this phrase meant that only in the church were the sacraments that were necessary for salvation properly administered and received, Hubmaier associated salvation with the church because of the church's instructional and shepherding role, performed by means of its utilization of the keys, which were, in turn, intimately connected to church discipline. Thus, the importance of Hubmaier's doctrine of church discipline extends also to his understanding of sanctification, which was discussed in the reformer's writings as the second stage of justification. To summarize the consequence of Hubmaier's church discipline to his soteriology—it was the former doctrine that enabled the Anabaptist leader to keep the proper tension between human responsibility and divine action in his understanding of salvation, without falling into either the works-based justification of the Catholic Church, or, from his perspective, the incomplete understanding of salvation of the Magisterial Reformers and aided the believers in their growth in sanctification by providing built-in accountability within the local body.

The fourth and final discovery is regarding that of the genius of Balthasar Hubmaier's organization of theology. As this research strived to make evident, Hubmaier was able to ground his theology in praxis via the doctrine of church discipline. In doing so, he bridged the gap, which

---

33. Hubmaier, "Freedom, I," 429; Hubmaier, "Schriften," 381.

is still in existence in many churches today "between the theory and the practice of convenantal membership," states Maurice Martin.[34]

To be more specific, the purpose of Hubmaier's church discipline, as mentioned earlier in this work, was fourfold, the first three of which were documented prior to this dissertation: first, to keep the church pure and unpolluted by shame before the outside world; second, to keep believers within the fold from stumbling and joining the offender in sinful pursuits; third, to cause the offender to repent and eventually be brought back into the fold. The fourth purpose of Hubmaier's doctrine of church discipline, which this research has strived to demonstrate, was to become the means by which his theology is grounded in praxis.

In accordance with the Scripture, therefore, Hubmaier, and the Anabaptists by extension, developed a two-step disciplinary procedure consisting of congregational admonition and the ban, the exercise of which was in direct relation to the seriousness of the offense. Congregational or brotherly admonition was the first step in the restoration of the straying believer. Here the process of escalation outlined in Matt 18:15–22 was closely followed, where, in most cases, only upon a threefold rejection of discipline, the ban was considered.

Consequently, the doctrine of church discipline was of extreme importance to the theology of Balthasar Hubmaier, particularly the areas of anthropology, soteriology, and ecclesiology. Hubmaier's church discipline not only intersected each of the aforementioned areas of his theology, it provided a connection between theory and praxis, as well as safeguarded the work of grace in relation to the parts of the reformer's theology that may have sounded "works-oriented."

As this work has endeavored to explore the import of church discipline to one of the greatest minds of the sixteenth-century Reformation, Balthasar Hubmaier, it is only fitting that its first, and now final encouragement be a statement from his own pen, "Let us with the help of God undertake fraternal admonition not only in teaching but also with the hand and in deed."[35]

---

34. Martin, "The Pure Church," 31.
35. Hubmaier, "Admonition," 376; Hubmaier, "Schriften," 340.

Bibliography

PRIMARY WORKS

Aquinas, St. Thomas. *The Catechetical Instructions of St. Thomas Aquinas.* Translated by Joseph B. Collins. New York: Wagner, 1939.

Augustine. "On Grace and Free Will." Translated by Peter Holmes and Robert Ernest Wallis. In *Augustine: Anti-Pelagian Writings*, edited by Philip Schaff. Vol. 5 of *Nicene and Post-Nicene Fathers*. Peabody, MA: Hendrickson, 2004.

———. "On the Grace of Christ, and on Original Sin." Translated by Peter Holmes and Robert Ernest Wallis. In *Augustine: Anti-Pelagian Writings*, edited by Philip Schaff. Vol. 5 of *Nicene and Post-Nicene Fathers*. Peabody. MA: Hendrickson, 2004.

———. "On the Merits and Remission of Sins, and on the Baptism of Infants." Translated by Peter Holmes, and Robert Ernest Wallis. In *Augustine: Anti-Pelagian Writings, vol. 5*, edited by Philip Schaff. Vol. 5 of *Nicene and Post-Nicene Fathers*. Peabody, MA: Hendrickson, 2004.

———. "On the Predestination of the Saints." Translated by Peter Holmes, and Robert Ernest Wallis. In *Augustine: Anti-Pelagian Writings*, edited by Philip Schaff. Vol. 5 of *Nicene and Post-Nicene Fathers*. Peabody, MA: Hendrickson, 2004.

Biel, Gabriel. *Epitome et collectorium ex Occamo circa quatuor sententiarum Libros.* Frankfurt: Minerva, 1965.

Calvin, John. *Institutes of the Christian Religion.* Edited and Translated by Henry Beveridge. Grand Rapids: Eerdmans, 1957.

Clement of Alexandria. "Who is the Rich Man That Shall be Saved." In *Fathers of the Second Century*, edited by Alexander Roberts and James Donaldson. Vol. 2 of *The Ante-Nicene Fathers*. Peabody, Massachusetts: Hendrickson, 2004.

Cyprian. "On the Dress of the Virgins." In *Fathers of the Third Century*, edited by Alexander Roberts and James Donaldson. Vol. 5 of *Ante-Nicene Fathers*. Peabody, Massachusetts: Hendrickson, 2004.

Erasmus, Desiderius. *Novvm Testamentvm.* Desiderii Erasmi Roterodami Opera Omnia Emendatiora et Avctiora. London: Gregg, 1962.

———. *The Praise of Folly.* 2nd ed. Translated by Clarence H. Miller. New Haven: Yale University Press, 1962.

Bibliography

Hubmaier, Balthasar. "A Brief 'Our Father.'" In *Balthasar Hubmaier: Theologian of Anabaptism*, translated and edited by H. Wayne Pipkin and John H. Yoder, 241–44. Scottdale, PA: Herald, 1989.

———."A Christian Catechism." In *Balthasar Hubmaier: Theologian of Anabaptism*, translated and edited by H. Wayne Pipkin and John H. Yoder, 339–65. Scottdale, PA: Herald, 1989.

———. "A Form for Christ's Supper." In *Balthasar Hubmaier: Theologian of Anabaptism*, translated and edited by H. Wayne Pipkin and John H. Yoder, 393–408. Scottdale, PA: Herald, 1989.

———. "A Form for Water Baptism." In *Balthasar Hubmaier: Theologian of Anabaptism*, translated and edited by H. Wayne Pipkin and John H. Yoder, 386–92. Scottdale, PA: Herald, 1989.

———. "A Public Challenge to All Believers." In *Balthasar Hubmaier: Theologian of Anabaptism*, translated and edited by H. Wayne Pipkin and John H. Yoder, 78–80. Scottdale, PA: Herald, 1989.

———. "A Simple Instruction." In *Balthasar Hubmaier: Theologian of Anabaptism*, translated and edited by H. Wayne Pipkin and John H. Yoder, 314–38. Scottdale, PA: Herald, 1989.

———. "Achtzehn Schlußreden." In *Schriften*, edited by Gunnar Westin and Torsten Bergsten, 69–74. Gütersloh: Mohn, 1962.

———. "An Earnest Christian Appeal to Schaffhausen." In *Balthasar Hubmaier: Theologian of Anabaptism*, translated and edited by H. Wayne Pipkin and John H. Yoder, 35–48. Scottdale, PA: Herald, 1989.

———. "Apologia from Prison." In *Balthasar Hubmaier: Theologian of Anabaptism*, translated and edited by H. Wayne Pipkin and John H. Yoder, 524–62. Scottdale, PA: Herald, 1989.

———. "Axiomata—Schlußreden gegen Eck." In *Schriften*, edited by Gunnar Westin and Torsten Bergsten, 85–94. Gütersloh: Mohn, 1962.

———. "Concerning Freedom of the Will (1527)." In *Early Anabaptist Spirituality*, translated and edited by Daniel Liechty, 21–37. New York: Paulist, 1994.

———. "Das andere Büchlein von der Freiwilligkeit des Menschen." In *Schriften*, edited by Gunnar Westin and Torsten Bergsten, 398–431. Gütersloh: Mohn, 1962.

———. "Der uralten und gar neuen Lehrer Urteil (Ausgabe I und II)." In *Schriften*, edited by Gunnar Westin and Torsten Bergsten, 224–55. Gütersloh: Mohn, 1962.

———. "Dialogue with Oecolampad on Infant Baptism." In *Balthasar Hubmaier: Theologian of Anabaptism*, translated and edited by H. Wayne Pipkin and John H. Yoder, 275–95. Scottdale, PA: Herald, 1989.

———. "Dialogue with Zwingli's Baptism Book." In *Balthasar Hubmaier: Theologian of Anabaptism*, translated and edited by H. Wayne Pipkin and John H. Yoder, 166–233. Scottdale, PA: Herald, 1989.

———. "Die zwölf Artikel des christlichen Glaubens." In *Schriften*, edited by Gunnar Westin and Torsten Bergsten, 215–20. Gutersloh: Mohn, 1962.

———. "Eighteen Theses Concerning the Christian Life." In *Balthasar Hubmaier: Theologian of Anabaptism*, translated and edited by H. Wayne Pipkin and John H. Yoder, 30–34. Scottdale, PA: Herald, 1989.

———. "Ein einfältiger Unterricht." In *Schriften*, edited by Gunnar Westin and Torsten Bergsten, 284–304. Gütersloh: Mohn, 1962.

———. "Ein Gespräch auf Zwinglis Taufbüchlein." In *Schriften*, edited by Gunnar Westin and Torsten Bergsten, 164–214. Gütersloh: Mohn, 1962.

———. "Ein kurzes Vaterunser." In *Schriften*, edited by Gunnar Westin and Torsten Bergsten, 221–23. Gütersloh: Mohn, 1962.

———. "Eine christliche Lehrtafel." In *Schriften*, edited by Gunnar Westin and Torsten Bergsten, 305–26. Gutersloh: Mohn, 1962.

———. "Eine Form des Nachtmals Christi." In *Schriften*, edited by Gunnar Westin and Torsten Bergsten, 353–65. Gutersloh: Mohn, 1962.

———. "Eine Form zu taufen." In *Schriften*, edited by Gunnar Westin and Torsten Bergsten, 347–52. Gütersloh: Mohn, 1962.

———. "Eine kurze Entschuldigung." In *Schriften*, edited by Gunnar Westin and Torsten Bergsten, 270–83. Gütersloh: Mohn, 1962.

———. "Eine Rechenschaft des Glaubens." In *Schriften*, edited by Gunnar Westin and Torsten Bergsten, 458–92. Gütersloh: Mohn, 1962.

———. "Eine Summe eines ganzen christlichen Lebens." In *Schriften*, edited by Gunnar Westin and Torsten Bergsten, 108–15. Gutersloh: Mohn, 1962.

———. "Etliche Schlußreden vom Unterricht der Messe." In *Schriften*, edited by Gunnar Westin and Torsten Bergsten, 101–4. Gütersloh: Mohn, 1962.

———. "Freedom of the Will, I." In *Balthasar Hubmaier: Theologian of Anabaptism*, translated and edited by H. Wayne Pipkin and John H. Yoder, 426–48. Scottdale, PA: Herald, 1989.

———. "Freedom of the Will, II." In *Balthasar Hubmaier: Theologian of Anabaptism*, translated and edited by H. Wayne Pipkin and John H. Yoder, 449–91. Scottdale, PA: Herald, 1989.

———. "Grund und Ursache." In *Schriften*, edited by Gunnar Westin and Torsten Bergsten, 327–36. Gütersloh: Mohn, 1962.

———. "Interrogation and Release." In *Balthasar Hubmaier: Theologian of Anabaptism*, translated and edited by H. Wayne Pipkin and John H. Yoder, 160–65. Scottdale, PA: Herald, 1989.

———. "Letter to Oecolampad." In *Balthasar Hubmaier: Theologian of Anabaptism*, translated and edited by H. Wayne Pipkin and John H. Yoder, 67–72. Scottdale, PA: Herald, 1989.

———. "Letter to Zurich Council." In *Balthasar Hubmaier: Theologian of Anabaptism*, translated and edited by H. Wayne Pipkin and John H. Yoder, 90–94. Scottdale, PA: Herald, 1989.

———. "Öffentliche Erbietung." In *Schriften*, edited by Gunnar Westin and Torsten Bergsten, 105–7. Gütersloh: Mohn, 1962.

———. "Old and New Teachers on Believers Baptism." In *Balthasar Hubmaier: Theologian of Anabaptism*, translated and edited by H. Wayne Pipkin and John H. Yoder, 245–74. Scottdale, PA: Herald, 1989.

———. "On Fraternal Admonition." In *Balthasar Hubmaier: Theologian of Anabaptism*, translated and edited by H. Wayne Pipkin and John H. Yoder, 372–85. Scottdale, PA: Herald, 1989.

———. "On Free Will." In *Spiritual and Anabaptist Writers*, edited by George H. Williams and Angel M. Mergal, 112–35. Philadelphia: Westminster, 1958.

———. "On Heretics and Those Who Burn Them." In *Balthasar Hubmaier: Theologian of Anabaptism*, translated and edited by H. Wayne Pipkin and John H. Yoder, 58–66. Scottdale, PA: Herald, 1989.

———. "On the Christian Ban." In *Balthasar Hubmaier: Theologian of Anabaptism*, translated and edited by H. Wayne Pipkin and John H. Yoder, 409–25. Scottdale, PA: Herald, 1989.

———. "On the Christian Ban." In *Three Reformation Catechisms: Catholic, Anabaptist, Lutheran*, translated by Denis Janz, 409–25. New York: Mellen, 1982.

———. "On the Christian Baptism of Believers." In *Balthasar Hubmaier: Theologian of Anabaptism*, translated and edited by H. Wayne Pipkin and John H. Yoder, 95–149. Scottdale, PA: Herald, 1989.

———. "On the Sword." In *Balthasar Hubmaier: Theologian of Anabaptism*, translated and edited by H. Wayne Pipkin and John H. Yoder, 492–523. Scottdale, PA: Herald, 1989.

———. "On the Sword." In *The Radical Reformation*, translated and edited by Michael G. Baylor, 181–209. New York: Cambridge University Press, 1991.

———. "Recantation at Zurich." In *Balthasar Hubmaier: Theologian of Anabaptism*, translated and edited by H. Wayne Pipkin and John H. Yoder, 150–59. Scottdale, PA: Herald, 1989.

———. "'Rejoice, Rejoice.'" In *Balthasar Hubmaier: Theologian of Anabaptism*, translated and edited by H. Wayne Pipkin and John H. Yoder, 566–71. Scottdale, PA: Herald, 1989.

———. "Several Theses Concerning the Mass." In *Balthasar Hubmaier: Theologian of Anabaptism*, translated and edited by H. Wayne Pipkin and John H. Yoder, 73–77. Scottdale, PA: Herald, 1989.

———. "Statements at the Second Zurich Disputation." In *Balthasar Hubmaier: Theologian of Anabaptism*, translated and edited by H. Wayne Pipkin and John H. Yoder, 21–29. Scottdale, PA: Herald, 1989.

———. "Summa of the Entire Christian Life." In *Balthasar Hubmaier: Theologian of Anabaptism*, translated and edited by H. Wayne Pipkin and John H. Yoder, 524–62. Scottdale, PA: Herald, 1989.

———. "Testimony in Vienna." In *Balthasar Hubmaier: Theologian of Anabaptism*, translated and edited by H. Wayne Pipkin and John H. Yoder, 563–65. Scottdale, PA: Herald, 1989.

———. "The Ground and Reason." In *Balthasar Hubmaier: Theologian of Anabaptism*, translated and edited by H. Wayne Pipkin and John H. Yoder, 366–71. Scottdale, PA: Herald, 1989.

———. "The Twelve Articles in Prayer Form." In *Balthasar Hubmaier: Theologian of Anabaptism*, translated and edited by H. Wayne Pipkin and John H. Yoder, 234–40. Scottdale, PA: Herald, 1989.

———. "Theses against Eck." In *Balthasar Hubmaier: Theologian of Anabaptism*, translated and edited by H. Wayne Pipkin and John H. Yoder, 49–57. Scottdale, PA: Herald, 1989.

———. "Von dem christichen Bann." In *Schriften*, edited by Gunnar Westin and Torsten Bergsten, 366–78. Gutersloh: Mohn, 1962.

———. "Von dem Schwert." In *Schriften*, edited by Gunnar Westin and Torsten Bergsten, 432–57. Gütersloh: Mohn, 1962.

———. "Von der bruderlichen Strafe." In *Schriften*, edited by Gunnar Westin and Torsten Bergsten, 337–46. Gutersloh: Mohn, 1962.

———. "Von der christlichen Taufe der Glaubigen." In *Schriften*, edited by Gunnar Westin and Torsten Bergsten, 116–63. Gutersloh: Mohn, 1962.

———. "Von der Freiheit des Willens." In *Schriften*, edited by Gunnar Westin and Torsten Bergsten, 379–97. Gutersloh: Mohn, 1962.

———. "Von der Kindertaufe." In *Schriften*, edited by Gunnar Westin and Torsten Bergsten, 256–69. Gutersloh: Mohn, 1962.

———. "Von Ketzern und ihren Verbrennern." In *Schriften*, edited by Gunnar Westin and Torsten Bergsten, 95–100. Gütersloh: Mohn, 1962.

Irenaeus. "Against Heresies." In *The Apostolic Fathers with Justin Martyr and Irenaeus*, edited by Alexander Roberts and James Donaldson. Vol. 1 of *Ante-Nicene Fathers*. Peabody, Massachusetts: Hendrickson, 2004.

Luther, Martin. *Career of the Reformer I*. Edited by Harold J. Grimm. Vol. 31 of *Luther's Works*, edited by Helmut T. Lehmann. Philadelphia: Muhlenberg, 1957.

———. *Career of the Reformer IV*. Edited by Lewis W. Spitz. Vol. 34 of *Luther's Works*, edited by Helmut T. Lehmann. Philadelphia: Muhlenberg, 1960.

———. *Church and Ministry II*. Edited by Conrad Bergendoff. Vol. 40 of *Luther's Works*, edited by Helmut T. Lehmann. Philadelphia: Muhlenberg, 1958.

———. *First Lectures on the Psalms I: Psalms 1–75*. Edited by Hilton C. Oswald. Vol. 10 of *Luther's Works*, edited by Helmut T. Lehmann. Saint Louis: Concordia, 1974.

———. *Lectures on Galatians*. Edited by Jaroslav Pelikan and Walter A. Hansen. Vol. 26 of *Luther's Works*, edited by Helmut T. Lehmann. Saint Louis: Concordia, 1963.

———. *Lectures on Galatians*. Edited by Jaroslav Pelikan and Walter A. Hansen. Vol. 27 of *Luther's Works*, edited by Helmut T. Lehmann. Saint Louis: Concordia, 1964.

———. *Liturgy and Hymns*. Edited by Ulrich S. Leupold. Vol. 53 of *Luther's Works*, edited by Helmut T. Lehmann. Philadelphia: Fortress, 1965.

———. *The Bondage of the Will*. Edited by Henry Atherton. Translated by Henry Cole [on-line]. Accessed 1 November 2010. Available from http://truecovenanter.com/truelutheran/luther_bow.html#sover; Internet.

———. *The Christian in Society*. Edited by James Atkinson. Vol. 44 of *Luther's Works*, edited by Helmut T. Lehmann. Philadelphia: Fortress, 1966.

———. *Word and Sacrament*. Edited by E. Theodore Bachmann. Vol. 35 of *Luther's Works*, edited by Helmut T. Lehmann. Philadelphia: Muhlenberg, 1960.

———. *Word and Sacrament II*. Edited by Abdel Ross Wentz. Vol. 36 of *Luther's Works*, edited by Helmut T. Lehmann. Philadelphia: Muhlenberg, 1959.

Marpeck, Pilgram. "Pilgram Marpeck's Confession of 1532." In *The Writings of Pilgram Marpeck*, translated and edited by William Klassen and Walter Klaassen, 107–58. Scottdale, PA: Herald, 1978.

———. "The Admonition of 1542." In *The Writings of Pilgram Marpeck*, translated and edited by William Klassen and Walter Klaassen, 159–302. Scottdale, PA: Herald, 1978.

Zwingli, Huldreich. *Huldreich Zwinglis Sämtliche Werke*. Vol. 2. Edited by Emil Egli and Georg Finsler. Reprint. München: Kraus, 1981.

———. *Huldreich Zwinglis Sämtliche Werke*. Vol. 3. Edited by Emil Egli, Georg Finsler, and Walther Köhler. Reprint. München: Kraus, 1981.

Zwingli, Ulrich. *Selected Works*. Edited by Samuel Macauley Jackson. Philadelphia: University of Pennsylvania Press, 1972.

SECONDARY WORKS

Anderson, Stanley Edwin. *Your Baptism is Important*. London: Marshall, Morgan & Scott, 1960.
Armour, Rollin Stely. *Anabaptist Baptism: A Representative Study*. Scottdale, PA: Herald, 1966.
Averbeck, Richard E. "The Focus of Baptism in the New Testament." *Grace Theological Journal* 2.2 (1981) 265–301.
Baldwin, Thomas. *The Baptism of Believers Only and the Particular Communion of the Baptist Churches*. Boston: Manning & Loring, 1806.
Bax, Ernest Belfort. *Rise and Fall of the Anabaptists*. New York: Kelley, 1970.
Beachy, Alvin J. "Grace of God in Christ as Understood by Five Major Anabaptist Writers." *Mennonite Quarterly Review* 37.1 (1963) 5–33.
———. *The Concept of Grace in the Radical Reformation*. Nieuwkoop: De Graaf, 1977.
Bender, Harold Stauffer. "Baptism." In *The Mennonite Encyclopedia*, edited by Harold S. Bender, C. Henry Smith, Cornelius Krahn, and Melvin Gingerich, 224–28. Scottdale, PA: Mennonite, 1955.
———. *Conrad Grebel c.1498–1526: The Founder of the Swiss Brethren Sometimes Called Anabaptists. The Life and Letters of Conrad Grebel*. Goshen, IN: The Mennonite Historical Society, 1950.
———. "Discipline, Concept, Idea, and Practice Of." In *The Mennonite Encyclopedia*, edited by Harold S. Bender, C. Henry Smith, Cornelius Krahn, and Melvin Gingerich, 69–70. Scottdale, PA: Mennonite, 1956.
———. "Excommunication." In *The Mennonite Encyclopedia*, edited by Harold S. Bender, C. Henry Smith, Cornelius Krahn, and Melvin Gingerich, 277–79. Scottdale, PA: Mennonite, 1956.
———. "The Anabaptist Theology of Discipleship." *Mennonite Quarterly Review* 24.1 (1950) 25–32.
———. "The Anabaptist Vision." In *The Recovery of the Anabaptist Vision*, edited by Guy F. Hershberger, 29–56. Scottdale, PA: Herald, 1957.
———. "The Discipline Adopted by the Strasburg Conference of 1568." *Mennonite Quarterly Review* 1.1 (1927) 57–66.
———. "'Walking in the Resurrection': The Anabaptist Doctrine of Regeneration and Discipleship." *Mennonite Quarterly Review* 35.2 (1961) 96–110.
Bergsten, Torsten. *Balthasar Hubmaier: Anabaptist Theologian and Martyr*. Translated and edited by W. R. Estep, Jr. Valley Forge, PA: Judson, 1978.
———. *Balthasar Hubmaier, Seine Stellung zu Reformation und Täufertum, 1521–1528*. Kassel: Oncken, 1961.
Biesecker-Mast, Gerald J. "Spiritual Knowledge, Carnal Obedience, and Anabaptist Discipleship." *Mennonite Quarterly Review* 71.2 (1997) 201–26.
Blanke, Fritz. "Anabaptism and the Reformation." In *The Recovery of the Anabaptist Vision*, edited by Guy F. Hershberger, 57–68. Scottdale, PA: Herald, 1957.
———. *Brothers in Christ*. Translated by Joseph Nordenhaug. Scottdale, PA: Herald, 1961.
———. *Brüder in Christo*. Zürich: Zwingli, 1955.
———. "The First Anabaptist Congregation: Zollikon, 1525." *Mennonite Quarterly Review* 27.1 (1953) 17–33.
Blommestijn, Hein, Charles Caspers, and Rijcklof Hofman, eds. *Spirituality Renewed: Studies on Significant Representatives of the Modern Devotion*. Leuven: Peeters, 2003.

Blough, Neal. "The Holy Spirit and Discipleship in Pilgram Marpeck's Theology." In *Essays in Anabaptist Theology*, edited by H. Wayne Pipkin, 133–46. Elkhart, IN: Institute of Mennonite Studies, 1994.

Boyd, Stephen B. *Pilgram Marpeck: His Life and Social Theology*. Durham, NC: Duke University Press, 1992.

Brewer, Brian Christian. "A Response to Grace: The Sacramental Theology of Balthasar Hubmaier." Ph.D. diss., Drew University, 2003.

Burkholder, J. Lawrence. "The Anabaptist Vision of Discipleship." In *The Recovery of the Anabaptist Vision*, edited by Guy F. Hershberger, 135–51. Scottdale, PA: Herald, 1957.

Burrage, Champlin. *History and Criticism. The Early English Dissenters in the Light of Recent Research (1550–1641)*, vol. 1. New York: Russell & Russell, 1967.

———. *Illustrative Documents. The Early English Dissenters in the Light of Recent Research (1550–1641)*, vol. 2. New York: Russell & Russell, 1967.

———. *The True Story of Robert Browne (1550?–1633) Father of Congregationalism*. Oxford: Oxford University Press, 1906.

Burrage, Henry S. *A History of the Anabaptists in Switzerland*. New York: Franklin, 1973.

———. *Religious Liberty in the Sixteenth Century*. Philadelphia: American Baptist Publication Society, 1892.

———. *The Act of Baptism in the History of the Christian Church*. Philadelphia: American Baptist Publication Society, 1879.

Caner, Emir Fethi. "Truth is Unkillable: The Life and Writings of Balthasar Hubmaier, Theologian of Anabaptism." Ph.D. diss., University of Texas, 1999.

Clasen, Claus-Peter. *Anabaptism: A Social History, 1525–1618. Switzerland, Austria, Moravia, South and Central Germany*. Ithaca, NY: Cornell University Press, 1972.

Coker, Joe L. "'Cast Out from Among the Saints': Church Discipline Among Anabaptists and English Separatists in Holland, 1590–1620." *Reformation* 11 (2006) 1–27.

Courtenay, William J. "Late Medieval Nominalism Revisited: 1972–1982." *Journal of the History of Ideas* 44.1 (1983) 159–64.

———. "Nominalism and Late Medieval Religion." In *The Pursuit of Holiness in Late Medieval and Renaissance Religion*, edited by Charles Trinkaus and Heiko A. Oberman, 26–58. Leiden: Brill, 1974.

———. "The King and the Leaden Coin: The Economic Background of Sine Qua Non Causality." *Traditio* 28 (1972) 185–209.

Cross, Anthony R. *Baptism and the Baptists*. Carlisle, U.K.: Paternoster, 2000.

Davis, Kenneth Ronald. *Anabaptism and Asceticism*. Scottdale, PA: Herald, 1974.

———. "Erasmus As a Progenitor of Anabaptist Theology and Piety." *Mennonite Quarterly Review* 47.3 (1973) 163–78.

———. "No Discipline, No Church: An Anabaptist Contribution to the Reformed Tradition." *The Sixteenth Century Journal* 13.4 (1982) 43–58.

Denning, Carl Elvin. "The Life and Teachings of Balthasar Hubmaier." B.D. thesis, Northern Baptist Theological Seminary, 1945.

Ditzler, J. *Baptism*. Nashville, TN: Publishing House of the M. E. Church, 1895.

Dueck, Al. "Story, Community and Ritual: Anabaptist Themes and Mental Health." *Mennonite Quarterly Review* 63.1 (1989) 77–91.

Dyck, Cornelius J. "Life of the Spirit in Anabaptism." *Mennonite Quarterly Review* 47.4 (1973) 309–26.

Bibliography

Erikson, Millard J. "The Lord's Supper." In *The People of God: Essays on the Believers' Church*, edited by Paul Basden and David S. Dockery, 51–62. Nashville: Broadman Press, 1991.

Estep, William Roscoe. "Anabaptist View of Salvation." *Southwestern Journal of Theology* 20.2 (1978) 32–49.

———. *The Anabaptist Story*. Grand Rapids: Eerdmans, 1963.

Fast, Heinold. "Dependence of the First Anabaptists on Luther, Erasmus, and Zwingli." *Mennonite Quarterly Review* 30.2 (1956) 104–19.

Finger, Thomas N. *A Contemporary Anabaptist Theology*. Downers Grove, IL: InterVarsity Press, 2004.

Foster, Jr., Claude R. "The Strasbourg Radical Reformation as Seen in the Works of Two of Its Leaders, Johannes Buenderlin And Pilgram Marpeck." M.Th. thesis, Crozer Theological Seminary, 1963.

Friedmann, Robert. "A Bibliography of Anabaptism, 1520–1630." *Church History* 32.3 (1963) 359–61.

———. "On Mennonite Historiography and on Individualism and Brotherhood." *Mennonite Quarterly Review* 18.2 (1944) 117–22.

———. "The Doctrine of Original Sin as Held by the Anabaptists of the Sixteenth Century." In *Essays in Anabaptist Theology*, edited by H. Wayne Pipkin, 147–56. Elkhart, IN: Institute of Mennonite Studies, 1994.

———. "The Oldest Church Discipline of the Anabaptists." *Mennonite Quarterly Review* 29.2 (1955) 162–66.

———. *The Theology of Anabaptism: An Interpretation*. Scottdale, PA: Herald, 1973.

Friesen, Abraham. "Baptist Interpretations of Anabaptist History." In *Mennonites & Baptists: A Continuing Conversation*, edited by Paul Toews, 39–72. Winnipeg, Canada: Kindred, 1993.

———. *Erasmus, the Anabaptists, and the Great Commission*. Grand Rapids: Eerdmans, 1998.

Fulop, Timothy E. "The Third Mark of the Church?—Church Discipline in the Reformed and Anabaptist Reformations." *The Journal of Religious History* 19.1 (1995) 26–42.

Garrett, James Leo, Jr. "Nature of the Church according to the Radical Continental Reformation." *Mennonite Quarterly Review* 32.2 (1958) 111–27.

Gilbert, Bill. *Renaissance and Reformation*. [on-line]. Accessed 2 November, 2010. Available from http://vlib.iue.it/carrie/texts/carrie_books/gilbert/index.html.

Gilson, Etienne. *History of Christian Philosophy in the Middle Ages*. New York: Random House, 1955.

Gonzalez, Antonia Lučic. "Balthasar Hubmaier and Early Christian Tradition." Ph.D. diss., Fuller Theological Seminary, 2008.

Graffagnino, Jason J. "The Shaping of the Two Earliest Anabaptist Catechisms." Ph.D. diss., Southwestern Baptist Theological Seminary, 2008.

Gray, Paul Wesley. "Balthasar Hubmaier." Th.M. thesis, Dallas Theological Seminary, 1975.

Haas, Martin. "The Path of the Anabaptists Into Separation: The Interdependence of Theology and Social Behavior." In *The Anabaptists and Thomas Muntzer*, translated and edited by James M. Stayer and Werner O. Packull, 72–84. Dubuque, IA: Kendall/Hunt, 1980.

Hall, Thor. "Possibilities of Erasmian Influence on Denck and Hubmaier in Their Views on the Freedom of the Will." *Mennonite Quarterly Review* 35.2 (1961) 149–70.

Harris, Murray J. "Baptism and the Lord's Supper." In *In God's Community*, edited by David J. Ellis and W. Ward Gasque, 14–28. Wheaton, IL: Shaw, 1978.
Hein, Kenneth. *Eucharist and Excommunication*. Frankfurt: Lang, 1973.
Hendricks, William I. "Baptists and Children: The Beginnings of Grace." *Southwestern Journal of Theology* 28.2 (1986) 49–53.
Hillerbrand, Hans J. *The Reformation: A Narrative History Related by Contemporary Observers and Participants*. Grand Rapids: Baker, 1978.
Hinson, E. Glenn. "The Quest for Integrity in Early Christianity: Third and Fourth Century Baptismal and Catechetical Procedures in the Shaping of Human Motives and Goals." *Perspectives in Religious Studies* 24.1 (1997) 49–64.
Horsch, John. "Hutterian Brethren 1528–1928: A Story of Martyrdom and Loyalty." *Mennonite Quarterly Review* 3.4 (1929) 254–73.
Jones, Rufus M. *Studies in Mystical Religion*. London: Macmillan, 1919.
Jürgen-Goertz, Hans. *The Anabaptists*. Translated by Trevor Johnson. London: Routledge, 1996.
Kinghorn, Joseph. *Baptsm, a Term of Communion at the Lord's Supper*. London: Bacon, Kennebrook, 1816.
Kiwiet, John J. "Anabaptist Views of the Church." In *The People of God: Essays on the Believers' Church*, edited by Paul Basden and David S. Dockery, 225–34. Nashville: Broadman, 1991.
Klaassen, Walter, ed. *Anabaptism in Outline*. Scottdale, PA: Herald, 1981.
———. *Anabaptism: Neither Catholic Nor Protestant*. 3rd ed. Kitchener, Canada: Pandora, 2001.
Klassen, Ryan P. "Wielding Two Swords: The Ecclesiology and Social Ethic of Balthasar Hubmaier." M.A. thesis, Providence Theological Seminary, 2005.
Klassen, William. *Covenant and Community*. Grand Rapids: Eerdmans, 1968.
Krahn, Cornelius. "Communion." In *The Mennonite Encyclopedia*, edited by Harold S. Bender, C. Henry Smith, Cornelius Krahn, and Melvin Gingerich, 651–55. Scottdale, PA: Mennonite, 1955.
———. "Prolegomena to an Anabaptist Theology." *Mennonite Quarterly Review* 24.1 (1950) 5–11.
Kreider, Robert. "Anabaptism and Humanism: An Inquiry into the Relationship of Humanism to the Evangelical Anabaptists." *Mennonite Quarterly Review* 26.2 (1952) 123–41.
Leeman, Jonathan. *The Church and the Surprising Offense of God's Love*. Wheaton: Crossway, 2010.
Leth, Carl M. "Balthasar Hubmaier's 'Catholic' Exegesis: Matthew 16:18–19 and the Power of the Keys." In *Biblical Interpretation in the Era of the Reformation: Essays Presented to David C. Steinmetz in Honor of His Sixtieth Birthday*, edited by David Curts Steinmetz, Richard A. Muller, and John Lee Thompson, 103–17. Grand Rapids: Eerdmans, 1996.
Lewis, Jack P. "Baptismal Practices of the Second and Third Century Church." *Restoration Quarterly* 26.1 (1983) 1–17.
Lightbody, Robert. "Pastoral Care and Church Discipline." In *In God's Community*, edited by David J. Ellis and W. Ward Gasque, 52–61. Wheaton, IL: Shaw, 1978.
Liland, Peder Martin Idsoe. "Anabaptist Separatism: A Historical and Theological Study of the Contribution of Balthasar Hubmaier (CA. 1485–1528)." Ph.D. diss., Boston College, 1983.

Bibliography

Lindsay, Thomas M. *The Reformation in Germany from Its Beginnings to the Religious Peace of Augsburg*. Vol. 1 of *A History of the Reformation*. New York: Scribner, 1912.

———. *The Reformation in Switzerland, France, the Netherlands, Scotland and England. The Anabaptist and Socinian Movements. The Counter-Reformation*. Vol. 2 of *A History of the Reformation*. New York: Scribner, 1907.

Littell, Franklin Hamlin. "The Anabaptist Concept of the Church." In *The Recovery of the Anabaptist Vision*, edited by Guy F. Hershberger, 119–34. Scottdale, PA: Herald, 1957.

———. *The Anabaptist View of the Church*. 2nd ed. Boston: Starr King, 1952.

Loserth, J. Graz. "Hubmaier, Balthasar." In *The Mennonite Encyclopedia*, edited by Harold S. Bender, C. Henry Smith, Cornelius Krahn, and Melvin Gingerich, 826–34. Scottdale, PA: Mennonite, 1956.

Ludwig, Josef J. "The Relationship Between Sanctification and Church Discipline in Early Anabaptism." *Evangelical Journal* 14 (1996) 43–58.

Mabry, Eddie Louis. *Balthasar Hubmaier's Doctrine of the Church*. Lanham, MD: University Press of America, 1994.

———. "The Baptismal Theology of Balthasar Hubmaier." Ph.D. diss., Princeton Theological Seminary, 1982.

MacGorman, J. W. "The Discipline of the Church." In *The People of God: Essays on the Believers' Church*, edited by Paul Basden and David S. Dockery, 74–84. Nashville: Broadman, 1991.

MacGregor, Kirk Robert. *A Central European Synthesis of Radical and Magisterial Reform: The Sacramental Theology of Balthasar Hubmaier*. New York: University Press of America, 2006.

———. "The Sacramental Theology of Balthasar Hubmaier and Its Implications for Ecclesiology." Ph.D. diss., The University of Iowa, 2005.

Macoskey, Robert A. "The Contemporary Relevance of Balthasar Hubmaier's Concept of the Church." *Foundations* 6.2 (1963) 99–122.

Marrou, Henri Irenee. *St. Augustine and His Influence through the Ages*. Translated by Patrick Hepburne-Scott. New York: Harper Torchbooks, 1957.

Martin, Dennis D. "Catholic Spirituality and Anabaptist and Mennonite Discipleship." *Mennonite Quarterly Review* 62.1 (1988) 5–25.

Martin, Maurice. "The Pure Church: The Burden of Anabaptism." *Conrad Grebel Review* 1.2 (1983) 29–41.

Merriman, Michael W. "Introduction." In *The Baptismal Mystery and the Catechumenate*, edited by Michael W. Merriman, 6–18. New York: The Church Hymnal Corporation, 1990.

McClendon, James Wm., Jr. "Balthasar Hubmaier, Catholic Anabaptist." In *Essays in Anabaptist Theology*, edited by H. Wayne Pipkin, 71–86. Elkhart, IN: Institute of Mennonite Studies, 1994.

McConica, James K. "Erasmus and the 'Julius': A Humanist Reflects on the Church." In *The Pursuit of Holiness in Late Medieval and Renaissance Religion*, edited by Charles Trinkaus and Heiko A. Oberman, 444–71. Leiden: Brill, 1974.

McDill, Michael W. "The Centrality of the Doctrine of Human Free Will in the Theology of Balthasar Hubmaier." Ph.D. diss., Southeastern Baptist Theological Seminary, 2001.

McGrath, Alister E. *Iustitia Dei: A History of the Christian Doctrine of Justification*. Cambridge: Cambridge University Press, 1998.

———. *Reformation Thought: An Introduction*. 2nd ed. Oxford: Blackwell, 1993.

———. *The Intellectual Origins of the European Reformation*. Cambridge, MA: Blackwell, 1987.

Mohler, R. Albert, Jr. "Church Discipline: The Missing Mark," 1–13, 2010 [on-line]. Accessed 16 August 2010. Available from http://www.the-highway.com/discipline_Mohler.html.

Moody, Dale. "Baptism in Theology and Practice." In *The People of God: Essays on the Believers' Church*, edited by Paul Basden and Dockery David S., 41–50. Nashville: Broadman, 1991.

Moore, John Allen. *Anabaptist Portraits*. Scottdale, PA: Herald, 1984.

Moore, Walter L., Jr. "Catholic Teacher and Anabaptist Pupil: The Relationship between John Eck and Balthasar Hubmaier." *Archiv für Reformationsgeschichte* 72.10 (1981) 68–97.

Mosteller, James Donovan. *A History of the Kiokee Baptist Church in Georgia*. Ann Arbor, MI: Edwards, 1952.

Moule, C. F. D. "The Judgment Theme in the Sacraments." In *The Background of the New Testament and Its Eschatology*, edited by W. D. Davies and D. Daube, 464–81. Cambridge: Cambridge University Press, 1964.

Muralt, Leonhard von. *Glaube und Lehre der Schweizerischen Wiedertäufer in der Reformationszeit*. Zürich: Kommissionsverlag Beer, 1938.

Muralt, Leonhard von, and Walter Schmid, eds. *Quellen zur Geschichte der Täufer in der Schweiz, I: Zürich*. Zürich: Hirzel, 1952.

Murphee, Bobby Warren. "The Theology of Balthasar Hubmaier." M.A. thesis, Golden Gate Baptist Theological Seminary, 1958.

Newman, Albert Henry. *A History of Anti-Pedobaptism, from the Rise of Pedobaptism to A.D. 1609*. Philadelphia: American Baptist Publications Society, 1897.

———. *A Manual of Church History*. Philadelphia: American Baptist Publication Society, 1933.

Neff, Christian. "Ban." In *The Mennonite Encyclopedia*, edited by Harold S. Bender, C. Henry Smith, Cornelius Krahn, and Melvin Gingerich, 219–23. Scottdale, PA: Mennonite, 1955.

Norris, Richard. "The Result of the Loss of Baptismal Discipline." In *The Baptismal Mystery and the Catechumenate*, edited by Michael W. Merriman, 20–35. New York: The Church Hymnal Corporation, 1990.

Oberman, Heiko Augustineus. *The Harvest of Medieval Theology: Gabriel Biel and Late Medieval Nominalism*. Durham, NC: Labyrinth, 1983.

———. "The Shape of Late Medieval Thought: The Birthpangs of the Modern Era." In *The Pursuit of Holiness in Late Medieval and Renaissance Religion*, edited by Charles Trinkaus and Heiko A. Oberman, 3–25. Leiden: Brill, 1974.

Packull, Werner O. "A Reformed-Anabaptist Dialogue in Augsburg During the Early 1530s." In *Radical Reformation Studies*, edited by Werner O. Packull and Geoffrey L. Dipple, 21–34. Aldershot, UK: Ashgate, 1999.

Patterson, Paige. "Learning from the Anabaptists." In *Southern Baptist Identity*, edited by David S. Dockery, 123–38. Wheaton: Crossway, 2009.

Peachey, Paul. "Anabaptism and Church Organization." *Mennonite Quarterly Review* 30.3 (1956) 213–28.

———. "Social Background and Social Philosophy of the Swiss Anabaptists, 1525–1540." *Mennonite Quarterly Review* 28.2 (1954) 102–27.

Pelikan, Jaroslav. *Reformation of Church and Dogma (1300–1700)*. Vol. 4 of *The Christian Tradition: A History of the Development of Doctrine*. Chicago: University of Chicago Press, 1984.

Pieper, Josef. *Scholasticism: Personalities and Problems of Medieval Philosophy*. Translated by Richard and Clara Winston. New York: Pantheon, 1960.

Pike, Edward Carey. *The Story of the Anabaptists*. London: National Council of Evangelical Free Churches, 1904.

Pipkin, H. Wayne. "The Baptismal Theology of Balthasar Hubmaier." In *Essays in Anabaptist Theology*, edited by H. Wayne Pipkin, 87–110. Elkhart, IN: Institute of Mennonite Studies, 1994.

Pipkin, H. Wayne, and John H. Yoder, translators and editors. *Balthasar Hubmaier: Theologian of Anabaptism*. Scottdale, PA: Herald, 1989.

Rauert, Matthias H. "'Ein schon lustig Buchlein': The Influence of Pilgram Marpeck's 'Admonition' on True Baptism and Communion in a Hutterite Polemic." *Mennonite Quarterly Review* 83.3 (2009) 425–70.

Reimer, A. James. "From Denominational Apologetics to Social History and Systematic Theology: Recent Developments in Early Anabaptist Studies." *Religious Studies Review* 29.3 (2003) 235–40.

Rempel, John D. *The Lord's Supper in Anabaptism*. Scottdale, PA: Herald, 1993.

Roth, John D. "Harmonizing the Scriptures: Swiss Brethren Understandings of the Relationship Between the Old and New Testament During the Last Half of the Sixteenth Century." In *Radical Reformation Studies*, edited by Werner O. Packull and Geoffrey L. Dipple, 35–52. Aldershot, UK: Ashgate, 1999.

Rothkegel, Martin. "Anabaptism in Moravia and Silesia." In *A Companion to Anabaptism and Spiritualism, 1521–1700*, edited by John D. Roth and James M. Stayer, 163–216. Leiden: Brill, 2007.

Runzo, Jean. "Communal Discipline in the Early Anabaptist Communities of Switzerland, Germany, Austria, and Moravia, 1525–1552." *Mennonite Quarterly Review* 53.1 (1979) 78–79.

Sawatsky, Walter. "Russian Mennonites and Baptists." In *Mennonites and Baptists: A Continuing Conversation*, edited by Paul Toews, 97–112. Winnipeg, Canada: Kindred, 1993.

Schaff, Philip. *History of the Reformation: 1517–1648*. History of the Christian Church. Peabody, MA: Hendrickson, 1996.

Schilling, Heinz. "'History of Crime' or 'History of Sin'? Some Reflections on the Social History of Early Modern Church Discipline." In *Politics and Society in Reformation Europe*, edited by E. I. Kouri and Tom Scott, 289–310. New York: St. Martin's, 1987.

Seeberg, Reinhold. *The History of Doctrines*. Translated by Charles E. Hay. Grand Rapids: Baker, 1977.

Smith, Gregory Michael. "Forming a Community or Conforming to Unity?" *Religious Education* 72.3 (1977) 323–31.

Smucker, Donovan E. "The Theological Triumph of the Early Anabaptist-Mennonites: The Rediscovery of Biblical Theology in Paradox." *Mennonite Quarterly Review* 19.1 (1945) 5–26.

Snyder, C. Arnold. *Anabaptist History and Theology: Revised Student Edition*. Kitchener, Canada: Pandora, 1997.

———. "Beyond Polygenesis: Recovering the Unity and Diversity of Anabaptist Theology." In *Essays in Anabaptist Theology*, edited by H. Wayne Pipkin, 1–33. Elkhart, IN: Institute of Mennonite Studies, 1994.

———. "Swiss Anabaptism: The Beginnings." In *A Companion to Anabaptism and Spiritualism, 1521–1700*, edited by John D. Roth and James M. Stayer, 45–82. Leiden: Brill, 2007.

Stassen, Glen H. "Preparing Candidates for Baptism." *Review & Expositor* 80.2 (1983) 245–60.

Stayer, James M., and Werner O. Packull, eds. *The Anabaptists and Thomas Müntzer*. Translated by James M. Stayer and Werner O. Packull. Dubuque, Iowa: Kendall/Hunt, 1980.

Steinmetz, David C. *Luther in Context*. Grand Rapids: Baker, 1995.

———. "Luther und Hubmaier im Streit um die Freiheit des menschlichen Willens." *Evangelische Theologie* 43.6 (1983) 512–26.

———. *Reformers in the Wings: From Geiler von Kausersberg to Theodore Beza*. 2nd ed. Oxford: Oxford University Press, 2001.

———. "Scholasticism and Radical Reform: Nominalist Motifs in the Theology of Balthasar Hubmaier." *Mennonite Quarterly Review* 45.2 (1974) 123–44.

Toews, John B. "Baptists and Mennonite Brethren in Russia (1790–1930)." In *Mennonites and Baptists: A Continuing Conversation*, edited by Paul Toews, 81–96. Winnipeg, Canada: Kindred, 1993.

Trinkaus, Charles. "The Religious Thought of the Italian Humanists, and the Reformers: Anticipation or Autonomy?" In *The Pursuit of Holiness in Late Medieval and Renaissance Religion*, edited by Charles Trinkaus and Heiko A. Oberman, 339–66. Leiden: Brill, 1974.

Vedder, Henry C. *Balthasar Hubmaier: The Leader of the Anabaptists*. New York: Putnam, 1905.

Verduin, Leonard. *The Reformers and Their Stepchildren*. Grand Rapids: Eerdmans, 1964.

Vignaux, Paul. *Nominalisme Au XIVe Siècle*. Paris: Vrin, 1948.

Walker, Williston, Richard A. Norris, David W. Lotz, and Robert T. Handy. *A History of the Christian Church*. New York: Scribner, 1985.

Waltner, Erland. "The Anabaptist Conception of the Church." *Mennonite Quarterly Review* 25.1 (1951) 5–16.

Wardin, Albert W., Jr. "Mennonite Brethren and German Baptists in Russia." In *Mennonites and Baptists: A Continuing Conversation*, edited by Paul Toews, 97–112. Winnipeg, Canada: Kindred, 1993.

Warfield, Benjamin Breckinridge. *Calvin and Augustine*. Edited by Samuel G. Craig. Philadelphia: Presbyterian and Reformed, 1956.

Wenger, John C. "Grace and Discipleship in Anabaptism." *Mennonite Quarterly Review* 35.1 (1961) 50–69.

West, W. M. S. "The Anabaptists and the Rise of the Baptist Movement." In *Christian Baptism*, edited by Alec Gilmore, 223–72. Chicago: Judson Press, 1959.

Westin, Gunnar, and Torsten Bergsten, eds. *Balthasar Hubmaier Schriften*. Gutersloh: Mohn, 1962.

White, Charles Edward. "'Concerning Earnest Christians': A Newly Discovered Letter of Martin Luther." *Currents in Theology and Mission* 10.5 (1983) 273–82.

Wray, Frank J. "The Anabaptist Doctrine of the Restitution of the Church." *Mennonite Quarterly Review* 28.3 (1954) 186–96.

Bibliography

Williams, George Huntston. "Sanctification in the Testimony of Several So-Called Schwärmer." In *Kirche, Mystik Heiligung und das Natürliche bei Luther*, edited by Ivar Asheim. Göttingen: Vandenhoeck & Ruprecht, 1969.

———. *The Radical Reformation*. Vol. 15 of *Sixteenth Century Essays & Studies*. 3rd ed. Edited by Charles G. Nauert, Jr. Ann Arbor, MI: Edwards, 1992.

Williamson, Darren T. "Erasmus of Rotterdam's Influence Upon Anabaptism: The Case of Balthasar Hubmaier." Ph.D. diss., Simon Fraser University, 2005.

Windhorst, Christof. "Balthasar Hubmaier: Professor, Preacher, Politician." In *Profiles of Radical Reformers: Biographical Sketches from Thomas Müntzer to Paracelsus*, edited by Hans-Jürgen Goertz and Walter Klaassen. Scottdale, PA: Herald, 1982.

———. *Täferisches Taufverständnis, Balthasar Hubmaiers Lehre zwischen traditioneller und reformatorischer Theologie*. Leiden: Brill, 1976.

Wiswedel, Wilhelm. "The Inner and the Outer Word: A Study in the Anabaptist Doctrine of Scripture." In *Essays in Anabaptist Theology*, edited by H. Wayne Pipkin, 51–70. Elkhart, IN: Institute of Mennonite Studies, 1994.

Woodbridge, Russell S. "Gerhard Westerburg: His Life and the Doctrine of Purgatory and the Lord's Supper." Ph.D. diss., Southeastern Baptist Theological Seminary, 2003.

Wright, Nigel G. "Spirituality as Discipleship: The Anabaptist Heritage." In *Under the Rule of Christ: Dimensions of Baptist Spirituality*, edited by Paul S. Fiddes, 79–102. Oxford: Regent's Park College, 2008.

Yarnell, Malcolm B. *The Formation of Christian Doctrine*. Nashville: B & H Academic, 2007.

Yoder, John. "Turning Point in the Zwinglian Reformation." *Mennonite Quarterly Review* 32.2 (1958) 128–40.

Zeman, Jarold Knox. *The Anabaptists and the Czech Brethren in Moravia 1526–1628: A Study of Origins and Contacts*. Paris: Mouton, 1969.

Zijpp, N. van der. "The Conception of Our Fathers Regarding the Church." *Mennonite Quarterly Review* 27.2 (1953) 91–99.

Index

Adam, 33, 36, 42–43, 45–47, 61, 67, 98, 120.
Adelphi, Johann, 30.
admonition. See *congregational*
Aquinas, Thomas, 12, 31–33, 36, 39, 92, 129.
ambassadors, 46.
Anabaptist(s), iv, xi, 1–6, 8–14, 17–21, 23–26, 39, 41, 43–44, 48, 51–52, 55, 60–65, 67, 69, 71–73, 75–80, 82–87, 89–92, 94, 96, 98, 100, 102–3, 105, 107, 113–17, 119–21, 124–27, 130–32, 134–42.
Anabaptism, 2–4, 6, 8, 10–11, 13–14, 17, 20, 38, 46, 52, 62–63, 65, 72, 77, 82–83, 94, 103, 114, 117–18, 122, 125, 130–32, 134–42.
angels, 40.
Anthropology, vii, 2, 5, 16, 19, 24–27, 29, 31, 33, 35, 37–39, 41, 43–53, 67, 71–72, 75, 88, 93, 106, 117–18, 120–21, 127.
apostles, 15, 48, 90, 99.
apostolic, 83–87, 133.
Aristotelianism, 32.
ascension, 91, 106, 108, 118, 121.
assembly, 24, 87–88.
astray, 24, 114.
Athanasius, 16.
attribute, 57.
Augsburg, 6, 8, 138–39.

Augustine of Hippo, 35–36, 43, 55, 57–59, 71, 84, 125, 129, 138–39, 141.
Augustinianism, 27, 35, 37, 39, 55.
außbrechen, 63.
authentic, 83.
authority, 28–29, 47, 77–79, 92, 119.

ban, 1, 4, 22–23, 52–53, 67, 77–79, 90–93, 106, 114, 118, 121, 124, 127, 132, 139.
banishing, 23.
baptism, 2–3, 6, 8, 11, 14–16, 18–22, 24, 36, 48, 50, 52, 61, 66–67, 69–71, 74–75, 77–78, 83, 85–90, 92–108, 110–13, 115, 118–19, 121–24, 129–32, 134–35, 137–41.
adult, 2, 6, 11, 20.
of believers only, 11, 15, 21–22, 52, 70, 87, 90, 95, 97–98, 110, 119, 131–32, 134.
of infants, 8, 11, 15–16, 19, 21, 36, 86–87, 90, 94, 96, 101, 104, 130.
of the Spirit, 48, 75, 89, 96–100, 103, 122.
of blood, 97–99, 103, 122.
water 16, 21, 52, 77–78, 88–90, 92–93, 95–104, 110, 115, 122.
Basil, the Great, 16.
belief. *See* faith

Index

believer(s), 9, 15, 18, 21–23, 29, 52, 54–55, 59–61, 65–66, 70, 77–80, 84–85, 87, 89–90, 92, 94–98, 100–3, 106, 108–14, 118–24, 126–27, 130–32, 134, 136–39.
Bernard of Clairvaux, 5, 105.
Bible. *See* Scripture
biblical(ly), xi–xii, 23, 37, 39, 41, 55, 76, 78, 81, 84, 93, 99, 119, 122, 137, 140.
Biel, Gabriel, 12, 31, 33–34, 36, 39–40, 44, 51, 75, 129, 139.
bind, 13, 53, 77, 88–89, 92–93, 121.
birth, 13, 20, 38, 43, 47, 49, 64, 67, 75, 78, 97, 139.
blasphemy, 72.
body, 11, 36, 41–42, 44–45, 47, 52, 67, 83–84, 103, 107, 111, 115, 119–22, 124, 126.
bondage 22, 38–39, 69, 71, 93, 133
of the will, 22, 38–39, 71, 93, 133
Bradwardine, Thomas, 33, 35.
bride, 53, 91.
brother(s), 23, 52, 61–63, 96, 110, 112–13, 123, 134.
brotherly, 1, 4, 22, 52, 61, 63–64, 92, 96, 102, 114, 124, 127
brotherhood, 62, 79, 82–83, 100, 136.
bussfertigkeit, 63.

Calvin, John, 11, 37, 51, 55, 59–60, 75, 116, 129, 141.
Calvinist(s), 82, 85, 107, 123.
captive, 40, 46–47, 67.
catechism, 3, 31, 47–48, 63, 74, 77, 87–88, 93, 96, 101–2, 130, 132, 136.
choice, 39, 44, 46, 65, 79, 87, 105.
choose, 38, 42, 45–47, 52, 120.
Christian(ity), vi, 1, 3, 6–7, 10–13, 19, 22–23, 27–28, 30–33, 36, 42–43, 48, 50, 53, 59, 61, 66–68, 70–71, 73–74, 77–78, 83, 85, 87–92, 95–102, 104, 111–12, 115, 123–24, 129–30, 132–33, 135–42.,
church, xi–xii, 1–4, 6–7, 10–11, 13–14, 18–19, 22–24, 27–30, 32, 41, 51–56, 58, 60, 65, 67–69, 71, 76–93, 95–104, 106–27, 133–42.
church discipline, iv, vii, xi–xiii, 1–2, 4–5, 22–26, 51–53, 61, 63, 65, 76–79, 82–83, 88, 92–93, 102–3, 106, 112–15, 117–18, 120–27, 136–38, 140.
clergy, 27.
cognition, 51, 75.
communion. *See* Lord's Supper
commitment, 2, 12, 24, 61, 69, 75, 77, 81, 94–95, 97, 100, 102–3, 110–13, 117, 120–23, 125.
compulsion, 68, 73.
condition, 34, 42, 44–45, 53, 66–67, 69, 80.
congregation, 20, 52–53, 61, 78, 85, 92, 102, 108, 113, 120, 122, 134.
congregational, 22.
congregational admonition, vi, 1, 4, 22–23, 52, 75, 77–78, 92, 96, 112, 115, 127, 131, 133, 140..
connection, 7, 17, 24, 64, 81, 83, 93, 113, 124, 127.
Constance, Council of, 29.
council, 8, 28–29, 54, 80, 116, 131, 140.
conversion, 7, 18, 20, 55–56, 69, 89.
covenant, 13, 34–35, 40, 52, 94–95, 102, 111, 113, 122–23, 133, 137.
Cyprian, 62, 79, 126, 129.

darkness, 67.
daughter, 88, 121.
death, 7, 28, 42–43, 45, 50, 61, 66, 68, 74, 82, 98, 101, 103, 108, 110–11, 113, 119.
depravity, 70.

depraved, 50, 57.
destruction, 38, 52–53.
devil, 28, 50, 53.
devotio moderna, 27–28.
devotion, v, 7, 120, 134.
devout, 65, 99.
dichotomy, 64, 70.
disciple(s/ship), 9, 13, 26, 42, 60, 62, 64–65, 72, 75, 83, 91, 103, 111, 114, 122–23, 125, 134–35, 138, 141–42.
divinity, 46.
doctrine, iv, xi–xii, 1–5, 13–15, 19–20, 22–26, 29, 31–36, 38–45, 47, 50–55, 58–63, 65, 67–69, 71, 76, 78–81, 83, 86–91, 93, 96–97, 99–101, 103–8, 110–11, 113–15, 117–22, 124–27, 134, 136, 138, 140–42.

ecclesiology, vii, xi, 2–5, 24–25, 82–83, 87–88, 92, 103, 105–6, 118, 121, 124, 127, 137–38.
Eck, Johannes, 6–7, 12–13, 16, 27, 30, 37, 130, 132, 139.
effort, xii, 3, 20, 34, 45, 57, 83.
election, 59, 71.
enem(y/ies), 23, 43, 112.
enlightenment, 47.
  englightened, 48.
epistles, 7, 43, 46.
equitable, 57.
Erasmus, Desiderius, 3, 6, 12–21, 28, 30, 55, 66, 129, 135–36, 138, 142.
erbgerechtigkeit, 45.
error, 6, 10, 73, 80, 105.
Eve, 43, 45.
evil, 42–43, 45, 47, 50, 58, 73, 83, 96, 99, 112.
excommunication, 1, 22–23, 77, 79, 96, 134, 137.
executing, 23.
exegesis, 15, 42, 44, 50, 52, 74, 90, 137.

facere quod in se est. See synderesis
faith, 9, 11, 15, 18–21, 24, 28–29, 32, 37, 39, 48, 50–51, 56–65, 67–70, 72, 74–77, 82–83, 85–86, 88–90, 93, 96, 98–102, 104, 108–10, 112, 114, 119–20, 122–23, 125.
  acquired, 51, 75.
fanatics, 80.
fellowship, 21, 23, 61, 77–78, 88–89, 91–92, 101, 109–11, 113.
flesh, 23, 41–47, 50, 52–53, 61, 67, 98, 103, 107, 111, 121.
forbidden fruit, 44.
foundation, 55, 65, 78, 85, 93, 108.
freedom, 40–50, 53, 68–70, 72, 74, 79, 126.
  of choice, 44.
  of the will, 13, 16, 38–39, 40–41, 44, 46, 50–51, 53, 68, 73–74, 120–21, 125, 130–31, 136.
  unlimited, of God, 40, 51.
  limited, of man, 38, 40, 46, 95.
Friedburg, 6.
fromm, 63, 65–67.
Frombmachung, 65–67.

Gerechtmachung, 65.
Gesundmachung, 66.
glorification, 58.
good, 18, 28, 30, 34, 36–37, 42–47, 58, 60–61, 65, 67, 69–70, 72, 74, 93, 95–96, 109, 111–12.
goodness, 43, 47, 59–60, 67–68, 70, 109.
gospel, 15, 18, 22, 37–38, 40, 43, 60, 62, 65, 69–71, 89, 94, 100, 108.
grace, v, 3, 6, 34, 36–38, 40–46, 51–52, 55–61, 67–75, 78–79, 85, 94–95, 106, 109–10, 118–19, 123–24, 127, 129, 134–35, 137, 141.
  irresistible, 36, 73, 125.
  prevenient, 39.
grave, 61.

Great Commission, 13–15, 89, 96, 136.
Greek, 30, 45, 66.
Gregory, of Rimini, 33, 35–36.
guilt, 45.

health, 46, 67, 69, 135.
Hebrew, 30, 41, 45.
heterodox, 29.
Holcot, Robert, 33–34, 36.
Holy Spirit, xiii, 8, 15, 18, 36, 40, 46–47, 50–51, 69, 102, 108, 118–19, 135.
Hubmaier, iv, vi–vii, xi–xiii, 1–10, 12–17, 19–24, 26–28, 30–31, 33–34, 36–53, 55, 57, 60–81, 83, 87–127, 130–32, 134–42.
human, 26, 33–37, 41–43, 46, 50–52, 56–58, 67–69, 72, 74, 78, 94–95, 98, 106, 109–10, 118, 122, 124, 137.
will, 1, 3, 39, 93, 120, 125, 138.
responsibility, 39, 73, 81, 93, 126.
Humanism, 3, 13, 17, 27, 30, 55, 63, 120, 137.

illumination, 40.
image, 42, 91.
God's image, 38.
impart, 59.
imputed, 59, 125.
incarnation, 91.
incorruptible, 52, 121.
individual, 6, 14, 53, 57, 62, 69, 79, 82, 102, 107, 112, 118.
individualism, 62, 114, 136.
infusion, 36.
Ingolstadt, 7, 31.
innocence, 42.
institution, 16, 28–30, 61, 83–85, 90, 97, 101, 106.
intellect, 51, 75.

interdependence, 62, 82, 136.
irresistible, 36, 73, 125.

Jerome, 16.
just, xi, 11, 35, 49, 57, 64–67, 70, 77, 83–84, 91, 94–95, 105, 111, 113, 116.
justification, 2, 12, 22, 24–25, 28, 31, 34, 36, 44–45, 49, 53, 57–70, 75–76, 78, 80–81, 83, 124, 126, 138.
forensic, 22, 58, 67, 78.
justus, 67.

keys of the kingdom, 2, 23–24, 53, 62, 76, 81, 88–93, 104, 121, 124, 126, 137.
king, 9, 34–35, 43–44, 94, 135, 138.
kingdom, 2, 43, 47, 62, 67, 81, 83, 90–93, 104, 121, 124.

lament, 43.
life, v, 3, 6, 10–12, 15–16, 18, 20–21, 28, 30, 34, 42–43, 47, 52, 56–57, 61–62, 64–65, 67, 71, 75–77, 79–80, 82, 85, 87, 97–100, 102, 106, 109–15, 117, 119–22, 124–26, 130, 132, 134–35, 142.
loose, 53, 88, 93.
Lord's Supper, 3, 6, 21, 24, 77–78, 83, 87–88, 91–95, 102, 105, 107–15, 118, 123–24, 134, 136–37, 140, 142.
and church discipline, 112–13.
Luther, Martin, xi, 6–8, 11–13, 17–21, 30, 37–38, 51, 55–59, 71, 73, 75, 83, 96, 116, 119–20, 125, 133, 136, 141–42.

Magisterial Reformers, xi, 17, 24, 26, 38–39, 55, 58, 60, 65, 67, 70–71, 78, 80–81, 83–84, 90, 96, 99, 103, 126.

Major, John (of Haddington), 12, 31.
man / human, xiii, 1, 3, 7, 10, 12–13, 18, 24, 26, 33–37, 39, 41–48, 50–53, 56–58, 67–70, 72–75, 78, 81, 93–95, 98, 102, 106, 109–10, 118, 120–22, 124–26, 129, 137–38.
mass, 14, 27, 88, 132.
medieval, 26–27, 30–35, 37, 39–40, 44, 50–51, 55, 62, 75–76, 86, 92, 99, 120, 126, 135, 138–40.
Melanchton, 30.
merit, 47, 57, 79.
  meritorious, 44.
misery. See flesh
missionary, 9, 89.
monk, 56.
monogenesis, 13–14, 20.
mother, 79, 88, 95, 121, 125.

nature, 2, 5, 36–37, 40, 42–47, 51, 59, 64, 67–68, 79, 81–82, 85, 99, 105, 107–8, 117, 119, 121, 125, 136.
New Testament, 6, 14–15, 23, 41, 43–44, 66, 71, 81, 84, 86, 89, 120, 134, 139–40.
Nikolsburg, 8–9, 20.
nominalism, 12, 27, 32–34, 135, 139.

obedience, 6, 46, 64–65, 75, 77–78, 90, 99, 102–5, 125, 134.
Occam, William, 12, 31.
oil, 43, 70.
omnipotence, 74, 108.
ontological, 44, 65, 67.
ordo salutis, 70.
Origen, 16.
originator, 69.
orthodoxy, 29.

pagan, 22.
passage, 14, 42–46, 50, 52, 56, 58, 66, 68, 73, 99.

Pauline, 7, 17, 41, 43, 55, 71, 108–9, 121.
  theology, 24, 26, 58, 71.
Pelagius, 34–35.
penance, 92.
philosophy, 27, 32–33, 36, 136, 139–40.
physician, 66, 70.
piety, 12–13, 21, 27, 114, 119, 135.
pluralism, 54.
polygenesis, 14, 141.
pope, 18, 28–29.
potentia absoluta. See power of God, absolute.
potentia ordinata. See power of God, ordained.
power of God, 13, 49, 70.
  absolute, 13, 33, 39.
  ordained, 13, 33, 39.
practice, xi, 1, 9, 11, 15, 23, 60–61, 64–65, 79, 90, 93, 96 100, 103, 110, 112–14, 117, 120, 122–23, 125, 127, 134, 137, 139.
praxis, 23, 126–27.
preaching, 7, 18, 20, 37, 48–49, 51, 66, 93, 96.
precondition, 57–58.
predestination, 22, 36, 38–39, 71, 73, 93, 129.
predetermined, 59.
prerequisite, 68, 89–90, 96, 102.
prisoner, 44–45, 109.
proclamation, 40.
professor, 7, 12–13, 30, 64, 142.
promise, 18, 35, 40, 64, 75, 95, 102, 112, 122.
Protestant(s/ism) 1, 6, 10, 12, 17, 62, 78, 80, 82, 125, 137.
psychological, 44.

quickening, 89.

Index

Radical(s), 1–6, 9–12, 14–19, 21, 23–24, 26–27, 33–34, 38, 41, 44–45, 50–51, 59, 61, 63, 68–75, 77, 79–80, 83–87, 89–90, 92, 94–96, 98, 101, 103–6, 108, 110–11, 115–16, 119, 122–25, 132, 134, 136, 138–42.
realism, 32–33, 36.
reason(s), 7–8, 19, 21–22, 32, 39–40, 45, 54, 57, 63, 65, 88, 90, 93, 96, 101, 104, 106, 117, 121, 132.
rebirth, 38, 47, 49, 67, 97.
Rechfertigung, 49.
recognition, xii, 17, 28, 46, 78, 85, 98–99, 101.
redeem, 35.
   redemption, 45, 47, 72.
reformation, 1–6, 8, 11–14, 17, 19, 21, 25, 27–28, 30–38, 44, 54–60, 62, 68, 71–73, 82–86, 94–95, 103, 110, 116, 119, 127, 132, 134–40, 142.
   Radical reformation, 2, 4–6, 12, 14, 21, 38, 44, 59, 68, 71–72, 84–85, 94, 103, 110, 119, 132, 134, 136, 139, 140, 142.
regeneration, 30, 59–62, 65, 75, 89, 94, 100, 103, 105, 122, 134.
Regensburg, 6–8, 27, 30.
remnant, 84, 86.
Renaissance, xii, 13, 28, 30–31, 58, 71, 135–36, 138–39, 141.
repentance, xi, 18, 20, 69–70, 77, 79, 121.
respond, 19, 37, 40, 46, 51, 61, 69–70, 75, 120.
restitute, 86.
restoration, 23, 38, 42, 46, 61, 68–69, 97, 127, 137.
   restored, vi, 1, 67, 69, 79, 86–87, 126.
resurrection, 60, 65–66, 75, 77, 80, 91, 99, 101, 134.
revelation, 32, 40.

general revelation, 40, 46, 70.
revolutionary, 17.
righteousness, 36, 38, 42, 45–47, 56–61, 65, 114, 125–26.
   alien righteousness, 59, 125.
Roman Catholic, 6, 10, 12, 76, 83, 95, 119, 125.
ruined, 43, 46, 53, 67.
Rychard, Wolfgang, 30.

sacrament(s/al), 3, 5–6, 11, 19–20, 62, 76, 78, 90, 95, 105, 107, 115, 122–23, 125–26, 133, 135, 138–39.
salvation, 11, 22, 24, 26–28, 35–38, 43, 46–48, 50–55, 57–64, 66–68, 70–73, 75–82, 90, 95–96, 104–5, 107, 121, 124–26, 136,
   by faith, 21, 37–38, 40.
   by works, 38, 56, 68, 72.
Samaritan, 43, 47, 70.
sanctification, 2, 24–25, 53, 58, 65, 72, 78–80, 90, 95, 102–3, 105, 113, 117, 122–23, 126, 138, 142.
Sapidus, John, 16, 30.
schism, 28–29.
schola Augustiniana moderna, 33, 36.
Scholasticism, 27–28, 31–33, 55, 57, 120, 140–41.
Scripture, 8, 10, 17–19, 27, 37, 39, 41, 44, 46, 48, 55, 59, 65–66, 73–74, 76, 84, 90, 96–97, 108, 125, 127, 142.
Scotus, Duns, 12, 31–32, 36.
shepherds, 15.
shunning, 23.
sick, 45, 49.
sin, 22, 36, 41–44, 47, 50, 56, 65, 67, 69, 71, 74, 79, 91–92, 95, 98–99, 101, 107, 129, 136, 140.
   sinner, xi, 23, 36, 40, 56–61, 66–67, 70, 72, 79, 91, 97–98, 101.

sixteenth century, xi, 1, 12–13, 17, 19–20, 23–24, 28–29, 31, 43, 54–55, 62–63, 71, 79, 83–84, 94, 116–17, 119, 127, 135–36, 140, 142.
sola fide, 11.
sola scriptura, 11, 19.
Soteriology, vii, 2, 5, 24–25, 34, 36, 43, 53–55, 57, 59–61, 63, 65, 67, 69, 71–73, 75–81, 88, 106, 117, 124–27.
soul, 36, 41–42, 44–48, 52, 67, 120.
Spirit, xiii, 8, 15, 18, 36, 40, 42, 46–51, 60–61, 64–65, 69, 74–77, 88–89, 96–100, 102–3, 106–8, 118–19, 122, 125, 135.
spirit, v, 40–42, 44–48, 50, 52–53, 67, 79, 109, 120–21.
state, 10–11, 67, 85, 87, 125.
striking, 23.
struggle, 10, 50, 56–57, 65.
suffering, 42, 98–99, 103, 108–11, 119, 123.
Swiss, 2, 13–14, 21, 139, 141.
brethren, 20, 64, 134, 140.
sword, 9, 83, 91, 132.
synderesis, 34, 39–40, 51, 75.
systematic, 24, 31, 63, 80, 87, 119, 140.

teaching(s), 2, 15, 27, 29, 41, 48, 57, 64, 73, 83, 86, 90–91, 98, 108, 111, 127, 135.
teacher, 6, 12, 15–16, 27, 37, 87, 99, 125, 131, 139.
tension, 14, 41, 52, 81, 121, 126.
Tertullian, 16.
theolog(y/ical), iii–iv, xi–9, 11–17, 19–38, 41, 44, 46–47, 51–52, 54–55, 58–66, 69, 71–72, 75–77, 80–87, 90, 92–100, 103–8, 110–11, 113–23, 125–27, 130–32, 134–42.

baptismal theology, 3, 15, 21, 94, 97, 99, 104, 115, 138, 140.
tradition, 3, 9, 19, 36, 114, 135–36, 140.
transgression, 46.
treatise(s), 4, 9, 16–17, 22–23, 63, 66, 80, 87, 93, 95, 97, 104, 115, 117, 120, 123.
trichotomous, 24, 26, 41–42, 51, 75, 120–21.
Trinity, xiii, 42, 97.
trinitarian, 15, 42.
tripartite, 19, 25, 37, 41, 46.

union, xi, 3, 27, 85–87.
with Christ, 59–60.
universals, 32–33, 36.
university, 6–7, 12–13, 30–31, 34–35, 57, 92, 120, 129, 132–33, 135, 138–42.
unregenerate, 37–38.

via moderna, 33–36, 57.
victory, 61, 65.
voluntary, 51–52, 68, 73, 85, 121.

Waldshut, 2–3, 5, 7–9, 12, 16, 19, 24, 27, 43, 52–53, 63, 67, 74, 88, 94, 107.
will, 1, 2, 5–6, 12–13, 15–16, 22, 24–27, 33–34, 36–48, 50–51, 53, 55, 58, 61, 63, 66–71, 73–79, 81–84, 88–91, 93, 95, 97, 99, 102–4, 106, 108, 111–12, 117, 120–21, 125, 129–31, 133, 136, 138.
wine, 43, 47, 70, 95, 108, 111.
witness, 11, 47, 89, 101, 110, 117, 122–23.
Wittenberg, 17–19, 58.

word, xi–xii, 8, 10, 18, 24, 37, 39–40, 45, 47–51, 61–62, 65–66, 68–70, 74–76, 78–79, 87, 89–90, 97–99, 102, 105, 111–12, 119–21, 124–25, 133, 142.

works, xii, 2, 4, 18–19, 21, 23, 28, 34–35, 37–38, 45, 56–58, 60, 63–65, 67–68, 72, 74–75, 80–81, 87–88, 96, 99, 102, 105, 107, 109, 119, 124, 127, 129, 133–34, 136.

worldlings, 64.

wounds, iii–iv, 18, 42–43, 70.

   wounded, 43–45, 47–48, 66–67, 70.

wrath, 47, 56.

Zurich, 2, 8, 14, 20–21, 131–32, 134, 139.

Zwingli, xi, 8, 11–13, 16–21, 51, 59, 75, 80, 99, 116, 119, 123, 125, 133–34, 136.

Lightning Source UK Ltd.
Milton Keynes UK
UKOW040746170612

194577UK00008B/10/P